CLAUDIA ANDUJAR

The Tate Photography Series is a celebration of photography by artists in the Tate collection, presenting some of the most significant photographers in the world today. Each book focuses on an individual photographer and includes a specially selected sequence of images and an introduction by a Tate curator, alongside a conversation about each photographer's practice. These collaborations between artists and experts serve to enrich our understanding of photography and its connection to everyday life.

Each year the Tate Photography Series adopts a unifying theme across four books that addresses social, political and cultural issues of our time. The theme for Series Two is Ecology and Environment, featuring photographers who examine aspects of our relationship with the natural world, environment and changing climate.

While overwhelming hard scientific evidence seems all too easy to dispute and ignore, artistic approaches to considering our place in the world appear to be a more effective way to reconnect and change. Photographic artists, ever-curious, sensitive and attuned to noticing patterns, creatively document and mediate reality to help us see.

This series explores Richard Mosse's work in the Amazon rainforest, finding new ways to represent climate change; Chris Killip's Seacoal series in North-East England, where a community subsists on discarded fossil fuel; Lieko Shiga's series *Spiral Shore*, which documents and reimagines a coastal community in Japan's Miyagi Prefecture that was struck by the earthquake and tsunami of 2011; and Claudia Andujar's life work protecting the Yanomami, one of Brazil's largest indigenous groups.

Series Two

2:1	**CLAUDIA ANDUJAR**
2:2	**CHRIS KILLIP**
2:3	**RICHARD MOSSE**
2:4	**LIEKO SHIGA**

CLAUDIA ANDUJAR

Edited by
Tobias Ostrander

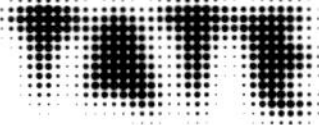

First published 2023 by order of the Tate Trustees
by Tate Publishing, a division of Tate Enterprises Ltd,
Millbank, London SW1P 4RG
www.tate.org.uk/publishing

A catalogue record for this book is available from
the British Library

ISBN 978 1 84976 866 5

Distributed in the United States and Canada
by ABRAMS, New York

Library of Congress Control Number applied for

Series Editors: Simon Armstrong and
Yasufumi Nakamori
Senior Editor: Nicola Bion
Production: Bill Jones
Picture Research: Emma O'Neill
Designed by Sarah Boris
Colour reproduction by Westerham Press, London
Printed and bound in the UK by Westerham Press,
London

Front cover: *Maloca surrounded by sweet potato
leaves, Catrimani* (from *A Casa*) 1971–6
Back cover top: *Vertical 8*, from *Marcados* 1981–3
(detail)
Back cover bottom: *Opiq+theri, Perimetral norte*, from
Sonhos 2002 (detail)

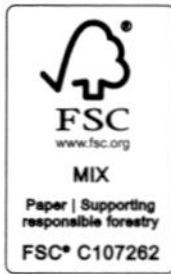

CONTENTS

6   **INTRODUCTION**

9   **IN CONVERSATION**

PLATES
16   **A CASA**
26   **MARCADOS**
40   **SONHOS**

64   **CREDITS**

INTRODUCTION

'Photographing is the process of discovering the other
and, through the other, oneself. Deep down, that's why
the photographer seeks and discovers new worlds, but
always ends up showing what's inside themselves.'
—Claudia Andujar

Claudia Andujar first met members of the Yanomami, the Amazonian
indigenous group of the Roraima region of Northeastern Brazil, in 1971.
This initial encounter led the Swiss-born, Brazilian photographer to
engage this community in a profound and on-going cross-cultural
interaction that continues to this day. Her photography captures
her personal and political commitment to the Yanomami, with her
activation of the medium shifting significantly over these past six
decades, as her knowledge deepened, and as the socio-political
urgencies of this community demanded different uses of her
photography. This trajectory moves from her technical experiments
during the 1970s, when she first began to live extensively with
the Yanomami, toward a documentary approach in the 1980s, as
she looked to use the medium in a more directly political manner.
Montage techniques appear in 2002, in her attempt to represent the
cosmology of the Yanomami. This formal and conceptual journey is
represented within this publication by three series, each of which has
strong examples held within Tate's collection, specifically the series
A casa, *Marcados* and *Sonhos*.

The *A casa* (The house) series presents images of *yanos* – large, circular structures with thatched roofs, that serve as collective homes for up to 400 Yanomami, and which are the centers of both communal and spiritual life. These images were produced in between 1971 and 1976, the artist's initial period of interaction with the Yanomami, years during which her status as an outsider slowly began to shift, as she lived for longer periods in the Roraima region. These photographs demonstrate Andujar's technical experiments, which included the use of long and double exposures, as well as smearing Vaseline onto her camera lens, to depict the magical lighting effects experienced within the interiors of the *yanos*. The artist also engaged infra-red film in the depiction of the exteriors of these architectures, which she shot looking down from high above them, or from low on the ground. The hot-pinks and intense yellows the film produces, combined with these dramatic shooting angles, give these homes an alien or other-worldly character. These technical innovations used in *A casa* help evoke a sense awe and wonder, emotional states that reflect the artist's developing relationship to this new context.

Marcados (Marked) are groupings of black and white photographs produced between 1981 and 1983, that depict Yanomami men and woman in starkly frontal poses, each with a numbered placard around their neck. The formal structuring of the images and the identification of humans numerically recall statistical depictions of concentration camp prisoners during the Holocaust. Half of Andujar's family were exterminated in Dachau and *Marcados* can be understood as directly seeking to relate her family history to the dire contemporary moment she was experiencing with her adopted family, the Yanomami. These images were originally produced by Andujar as part of a vaccination campaign pursued with several NGO's, fighting against the multiple diseases that had entered this community (which included malaria, tuberculosis, and measles), first through the attempted construction of the Trans-Amazonian highway and later through illegal mining in the area. The numbers placed on each person were intended to identify them for immunisation purposes, as the Yanomami do not designate permanent individual names. While as historicised referents these numbers evoke death and extermination, the artist has described the images as depicting individuals 'marked to live', a complex and charged use of these signifiers, one that formed part of her strategic engagement of her photographs during the 1980s into the 1990s, in her fight for the political autonomy of the Yanomami.

Sonhos (Dreams), the third and final series represented in this publication, was made in 2002 and consists of twenty photographs that were created by layering two or more colour negatives onto one another, all sourced by Andujar from her own archive. The montage effect achieved is dark and enigmatic, as images of humans and animals blend with those of trees, rocks, and rivers. *Sonhos* was produced during a period of relative political respite for the artist. In 1992, she and a group of activists had won a decades-long battle against the Brazilian government, which resulted in the federal demarcation of 96,000 square kilometers as protected Yanomami lands (an agreement currently under threat). Andujar has described her interest in representing the cosmology of the Yanomami with this series, an attempt she recognised as only possible after five decades of experiencing their unique understanding of the world.

The Yanomami believe that all material things are imbued with spiritual energies known as the *xapiri*. Demarcations between the material and spiritual realms are understood as porous and that these spirits can be called upon for guidance by their shamans, during ceremonies that involve smoking the bark of the *yãkoana* tree, which has hallucinogenic properties. Having witnessed these ceremonies and lived within this belief system of a non-binary flow of energy, Andujar looks to share this knowledge through these dream-like photographic constructions.

Tobias Ostrander
Estrellita B. Brodsky Adjunct Curator, Latin American Art, Tate

CLAUDIA ANDUJAR IN CONVERSATION WITH THYAGO NOGUEIRA

Originally published in the 2014 summer ('São Paulo') issue of *Aperture* magazine, the following conversation took place in February of the same year, between curator Thyago Nogueira and Claudia Andujar, as part of preparations for their exhibition *In the Place of the Other* that was held at the Instituto Moreira Salle São Paulo in 2015. After the initial period of discussions referenced here, the conversations and friendship between Andujar and Nogueira continued to develop, and together in 2018 they organised *Claudia Andujar: The Yanomami Struggle*. This large retrospective has toured extensively internationally, being presented at the Fondation Cartier pour l'Art Contemporain, Triennale Milano, Barbican Centre, Fundación Mapfre, Fotomuseum Winterthur, The Shed and, most recently, at MUAC in Mexico City.

TN   How did someone who was born in Switzerland and grew up in
        Hungary end up living in São Paulo?

CA   It's a long story. My mother was Swiss and my father was Hungarian.
        They lived in Transylvania, a place that was sometimes Romania
        and sometimes Hungary. For some reason – I should have asked
        why – she wanted me to be born in Neuchâtel, Switzerland, and so
        she went there for my birth. We then came back to our city, which is
        called Oradea in Romanian (in Hungarian it's called Nagyvárad). We
        lived there until World War II. In 1944, all the Jews were deported.
        My father was Jewish. He and his whole family were deported; they
        died in a concentration camp. I was living with my mother, who was
        divorced from my father. After he was deported, the Russians began
        closing in, so my mother decided to go to Switzerland. The rail trip
        took weeks because of all the broken bridges on the way. We also
        had to stop in Vienna, because my mother became ill. In the city,
        which was under German rule, my mother stayed at a hospital and I
        was interrogated daily. They wanted to know why we had fled. I had
        to hide the fact that my father was Jewish or they would have taken
        me. They never discovered my story. I stayed in Switzerland for two
        years, until one of my father's brothers found out that I was there
        and asked me if I wanted to come to the United States. I went as a
        refugee to New York in 1947 to live with my aunt and uncle.

TN   How was your time in New York? Why did you leave for Brazil?

CA   I didn't really get along with my aunt and uncle. They accused my
        mother of leaving my father. It's a complicated story … I decided
        to rent a room and go to work. I worked at the United Nations and
        I painted. At night I studied at the university. After a while I felt
        abandoned and married a Spanish refugee; that's why I have the
        name Andujar. But he became a soldier in the Army and had to go
        to Korea. I was really unhappy. At that time my mother was living in
        Brazil, where she had gone to marry a Romanian who ran away from
        the Russian occupation. After two years, my husband returned from
        Korea and we separated. I then decided to visit my mother. That's
        how I came to Brazil, in 1955.

TN   When did you take up photography?

CA   I abandoned my painting career when I arrived in Brazil. But I needed
        a language to communicate—for me, this was photographing people
        I met. I wanted to get to know Brazil because I felt at home there.

So I picked up a camera, and when I could, I photographed. I'm self-taught. I would go to the north coast of São Paulo a lot, and I began to travel to the islands of the fishermen and became friends with the families. What interested me were the origins of Brazil, the native population. I wasn't interested in the middle or upper classes

TN   Did you ever feel unsafe as a European woman traveling alone?

CA   No, traveling was easy. In the crowd I was mixing with, this wasn't a problem at all. I was adopted by the families of these people. I think that the connection through photography, showing the work to the people I was photographing, helped me identify with people and learn Portuguese. At that time, I met the famous anthropologist Darcy Ribeiro, and he suggested that I go visit an indigenous village. I embraced the suggestion and went to meet the Karajá Indians. Later, I tried to show my work to the Brazilian magazines O Cruzeiro and Manchete. But they weren't interested.

TN   Why?

CA   I was a foreigner, a woman who was messing with things she shouldn't. I stayed with the Karajá twice, two months each time. Then I decided to go back to the States to show my photography and was well-received. I went to *Life* magazine, to the museums. I had tried in Brazil, but nothing had panned out. In New York, I knew the world of photography. But I didn't want to stay in the States; I wanted to go back to Brazil.

TN   When you came back, you worked for the magazine *Realidade* (1966–1976), which was critical to the history of Brazilian photojournalism: the majority of their photographers were immigrants like you. What was it like there?

CA   The story of *Realidade* is special. The magazine's journalists were against the military government that took power in 1964; they looked for stories that spoke of the difficulties in Brazil. I did well there because the places I went were always places with people who were in some way oppressed by the political situation.

TN   You photographed stories on the erotic theaters in downtown
       São Paulo, childbirths, prostitutes in the countryside. What
       moved you?

CA   I was the person the magazine could always send to shoot
       in difficult places. I always sought out people on the margins.
       I wanted to get into people's souls. Later I got interested in
       the spiritualist medium Chico Xavier. There are things that to
       this day I don't understand. I would almost say that he had a
       connection with shamanism. But it isn't shamanism. He had
       a very strong spiritual life. The way he managed to do certain
       things – I can't explain it. Once I photographed someone
       being cured of cataracts. He hypnotised the person, gained
       some power over her, and stuck a knife into her eye.
       A knife! A regular knife, to cure her. And he cured her, but
       I don't know how this person kept quiet, leaning against
       the wall, and letting him do that. If I hadn't seen it, I wouldn't
       have believed it.

TN   You were also exploring the city.

CA   Yes, my photos of Direita Street and those made with infrared
       film are from that time, but those weren't for *Realidade*. I did
       those for myself. Before *Realidade*, I didn't photograph in color.

TN   You squatted on the ground to make the Direita Street photos.
       Did people find that strange?

CA   Well, they didn't find it very common; they thought it was a little
       curious, but nobody messed with me. They got a kick out of my
       attitude, that's for sure.

TN   Your 1970s work has a visual freedom that's rare for someone
       who worked for the press – the infrared film, the dislocated
       point of view, or even when you rephotographed slides,
       like in the photos of Sônia. Where did that experimentation
       come from?

CA   I would say that it was my contact with George Love, my
       second husband. He was interested in new angles, new ways
       of photographing. But even with these new techniques, I still
       maintained a humanist vision, don't you think?

TN   You once took a model and magazine crew to do a fashion
      shoot in an indigenous village. How did that come about?

CA   In the 1970s there was a fashion magazine called *Setenta*, for
      which I did various jobs. I suggested a fashion piece with the
      Xicrin Indians, which *Setenta* published.

TN   You were criticised severely for this piece, weren't you?

CA   I was – an anthropologist said I had gone to the Xicrin to
      show that they were inferior. For me it was nothing like that.
      I wanted to show that the Xicrin had their own style, their own
      inventiveness, that they were creative. But everyone has their
      own interpretation.

TN   In 1971, *Realidade* did a special edition on the Amazon.
      Why were they interested in the region?

CA   The Trans-Amazonian Highway was being built; an American
      had bought all this land there. When I went to photograph,
      there was so much deforestation going on. It was a disaster,
      but the Brazilian government allowed it to happen. They
      said that the Amazon was an empty space that had to be
      developed. The magazine was interested in showing what the
      Amazon was like at that time.

TN   Was it then that you made your first contact with the
      Yanomami?

CA   Yes. When I went to photograph in the Amazon, they asked
      me not to photograph the indigenous people because the
      Brazilian government was mistreating them. It was a type of
      government repression. But after I had been there for some
      time, I found out that a priest had died suddenly, and nobody
      knew how. I asked the magazine if they would be interested
      in this story. They said yes. So I went to the Yanomami.
      I never found out why the priest died, but I photographed the
      Yanomami. I liked them a lot, and in the end the magazine
      published many pages and put one Yanomami on the cover.
      The Yanomami hadn't received any Western influences yet;
      they were firstcontact people. The magazine accepted the
      story ... and we all forgot about the priest.

TN   *Realidade* had a short life span, did it not?

CA   After the special edition on the Amazon, they started letting
        people go. The whole office was fired for political reasons,
        because all of us were leftists. I decided to leave and no longer
        work in photojournalism. I decided to go deeper into the
        question of the Yanomami.

TN   So you went on to photograph them regularly, as an ongoing
        project?

CA   I tried to penetrate the Yanomami culture. I wanted to
        understand their beliefs, social practices, shamanism. I
        began this work in 1971. Later, in 1974, the government began
        the construction of the Northern Perimeter Highway, the
        second longest roadway in the Amazon. I was there when it
        began. And it changed me profoundly. I saw hundreds and
        hundreds of people dying. These people had no immunity to
        the diseases that were suddenly brought there. And, because
        of that, I decided to dedicate my life to their lives and culture.
        I tried to show the shamanism, which is essential to their
        culture. And I explored the contact and the harm this brought
        to these people, which was sickness and death. I used color a
        lot, and double exposures. I thought that I had found a kind of
        visual expression that referred to the culture.

TN   Therein lies the beauty of the work. You are always
        experimenting with visual language to deal with cultural
        questions.

CA   That's right.

TN   What was your routine in the village like? Did you take special
        precautions?

CA   In the beginning, they didn't know what photography was.
        When they first saw it, they didn't recognise themselves.
        With time I believe they will refer to the images I took of them
        as a reference to their past, their cultural heritage. But I
        think that to this day, it still isn't totally clear to them. I never
        photographed anything they didn't want me to. The death
        rituals, for example. They thought that through photography
        something of the person was stolen. In their funeral rites, they

destroyed and burned everything that linked the person to his life, to free his soul so he could live for eternity. That included burning the photographs.

TN   You received many grants to continue the work, including two from the Guggenheim, but in 1977, together with foreign anthropologists and researchers, you were taken by force from Yanomami lands. What happened there?

CA   I was ousted by the Brazilian government. They didn't understand what I was doing there. They thought I was trying to show how the government was mistreating the Indians. That I did this to show to people abroad, that I was some sort of spy.

TN   You've said you are not convinced your work in photography has been the most important thing you've done to date. What do you mean?

CA   Photography is an eternal search for myself – a language. But the work of trying to understand the life and the culture of a people is much more than photography. Photography is part of that, but not everything. One day we asked the Indians what art was for them. And they said we make our categories, and one of them is art, but for them it is not the same. Photography has brought me many things, but the survival of the world, of humanity, is something we struggle for constantly.

TN   Do you see a parallel between your story and that of the Yanomami?

CA   Yes, I do, of course. I lost my whole family and I always think my relatives were marked to die. I've learned so much from the Yanomami. We are destroying nature, destroying life. The Indians consider themselves part of this totality of nature, the human being as part of the whole. If you destroy any part of the whole, you destroy the world. That's why I did the photo of the end of the world in the series Sonhos Yanomami (Yanomami Dreams).

Thyago Nogueira is editor of Revista ZUM, a Brazilian photography magazine, and the head of the contemporary photography department at Instituto Moreira Salles, São Paulo.

A CASA (THE HOUSE) 1971–6

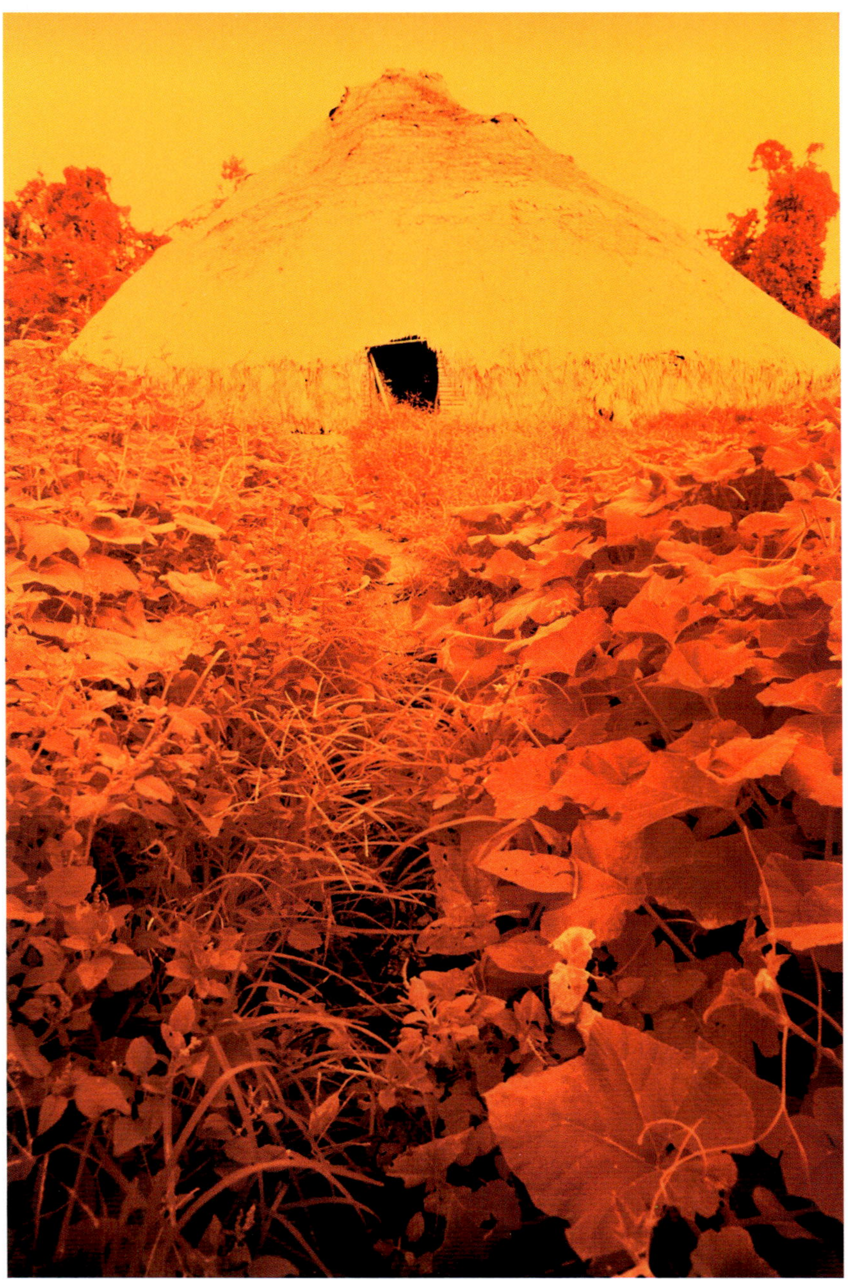

    Maloca surrounded by sweet potato leaves, Catrimani

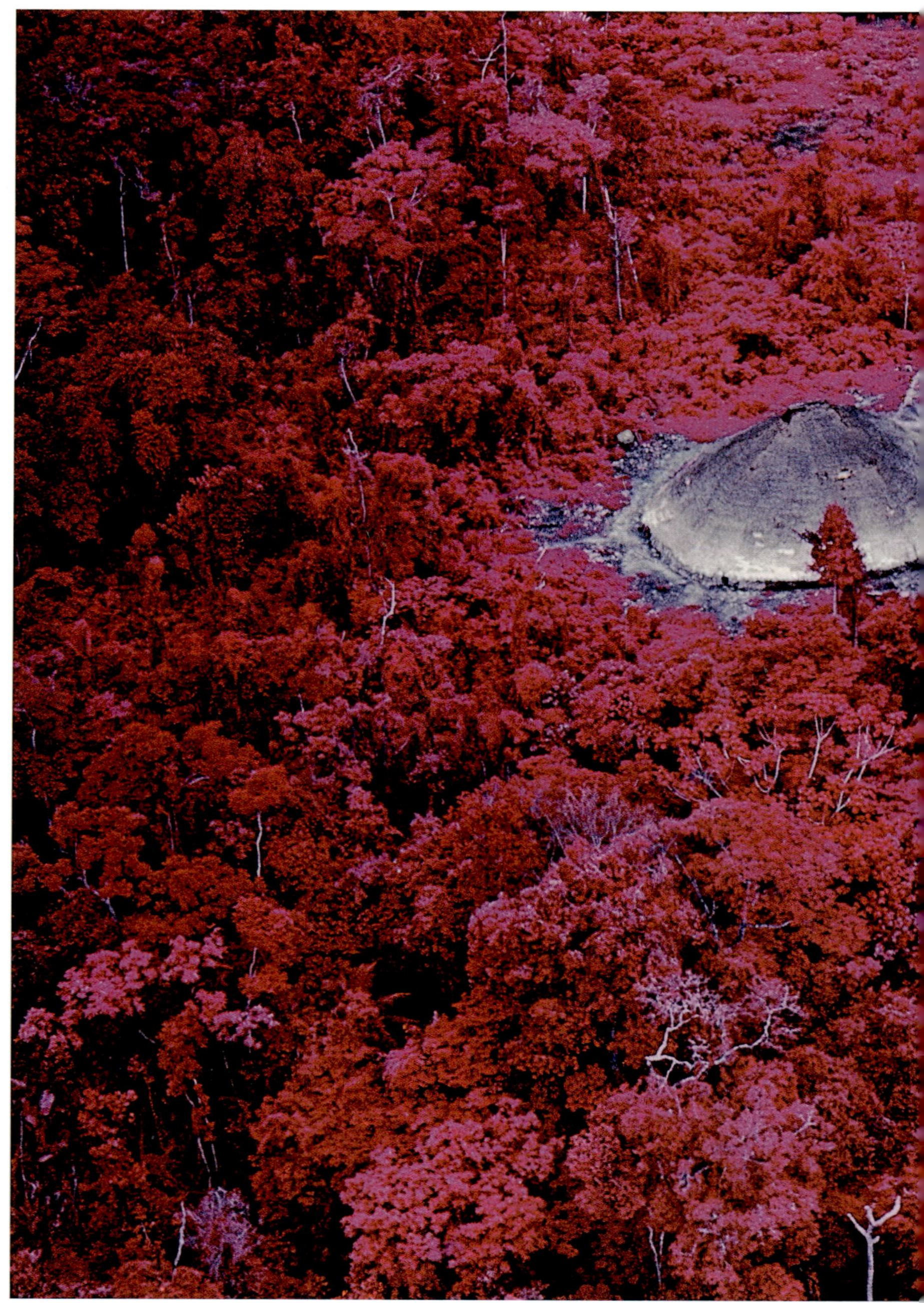

    Urihi-a

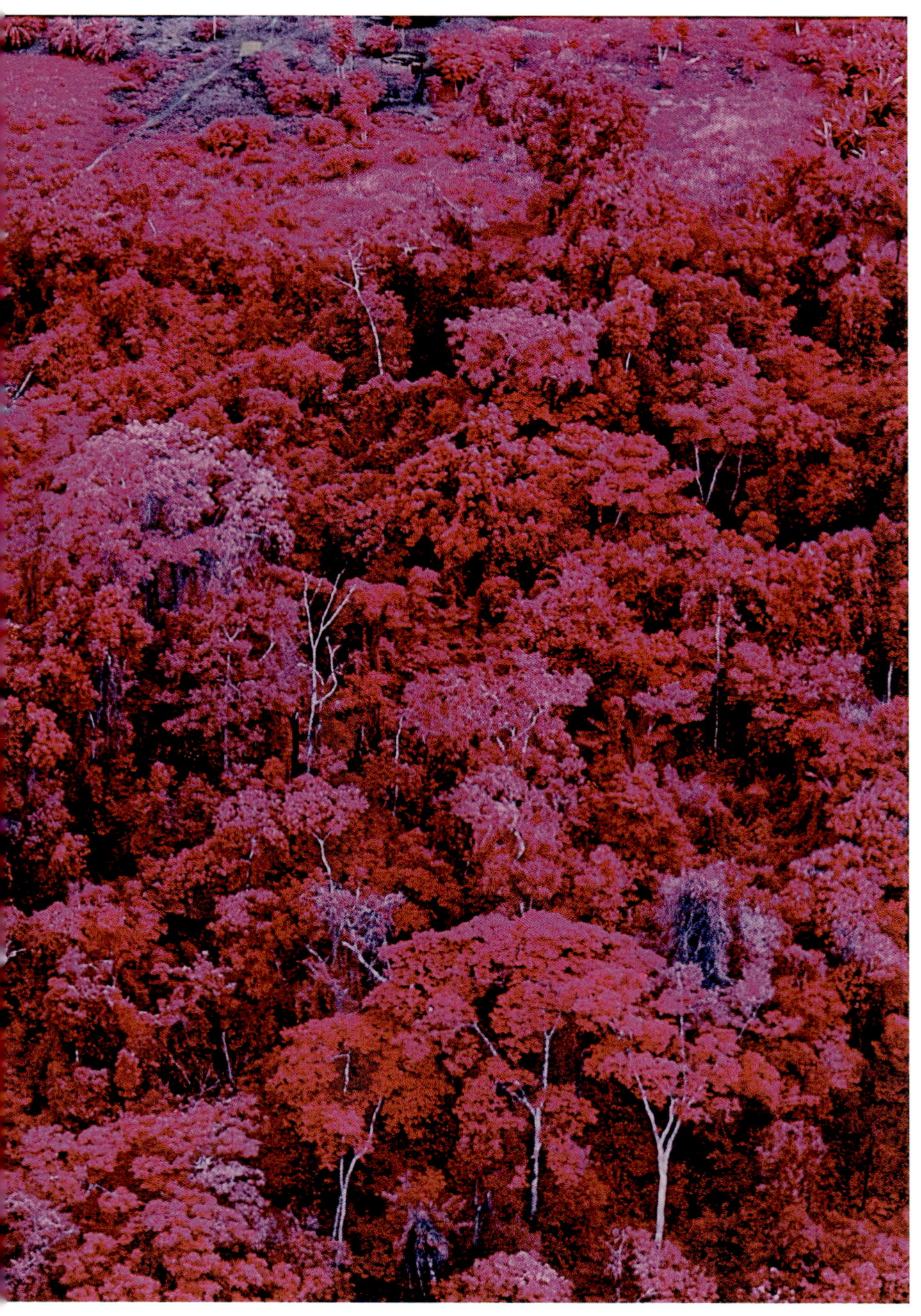

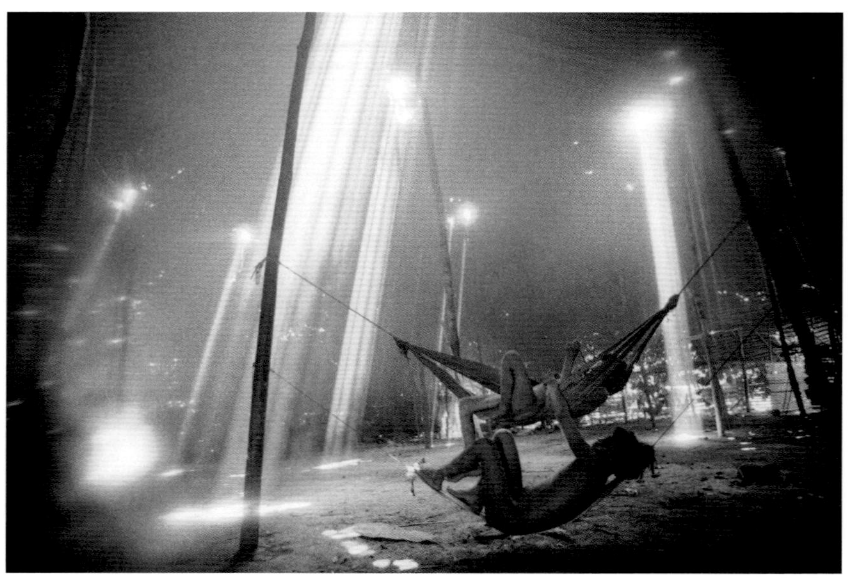

    Untitled 1974

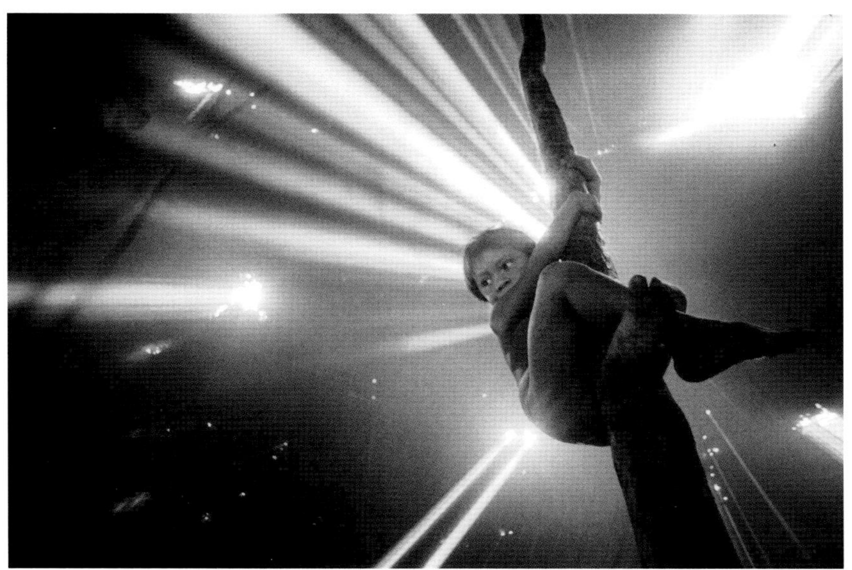

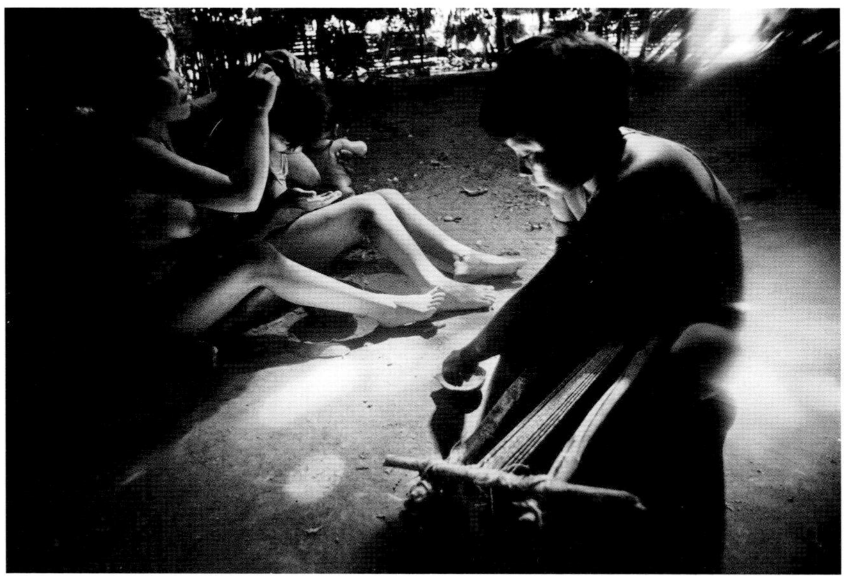

Top: Untitled 1974
Bottom: *Loom* 1975

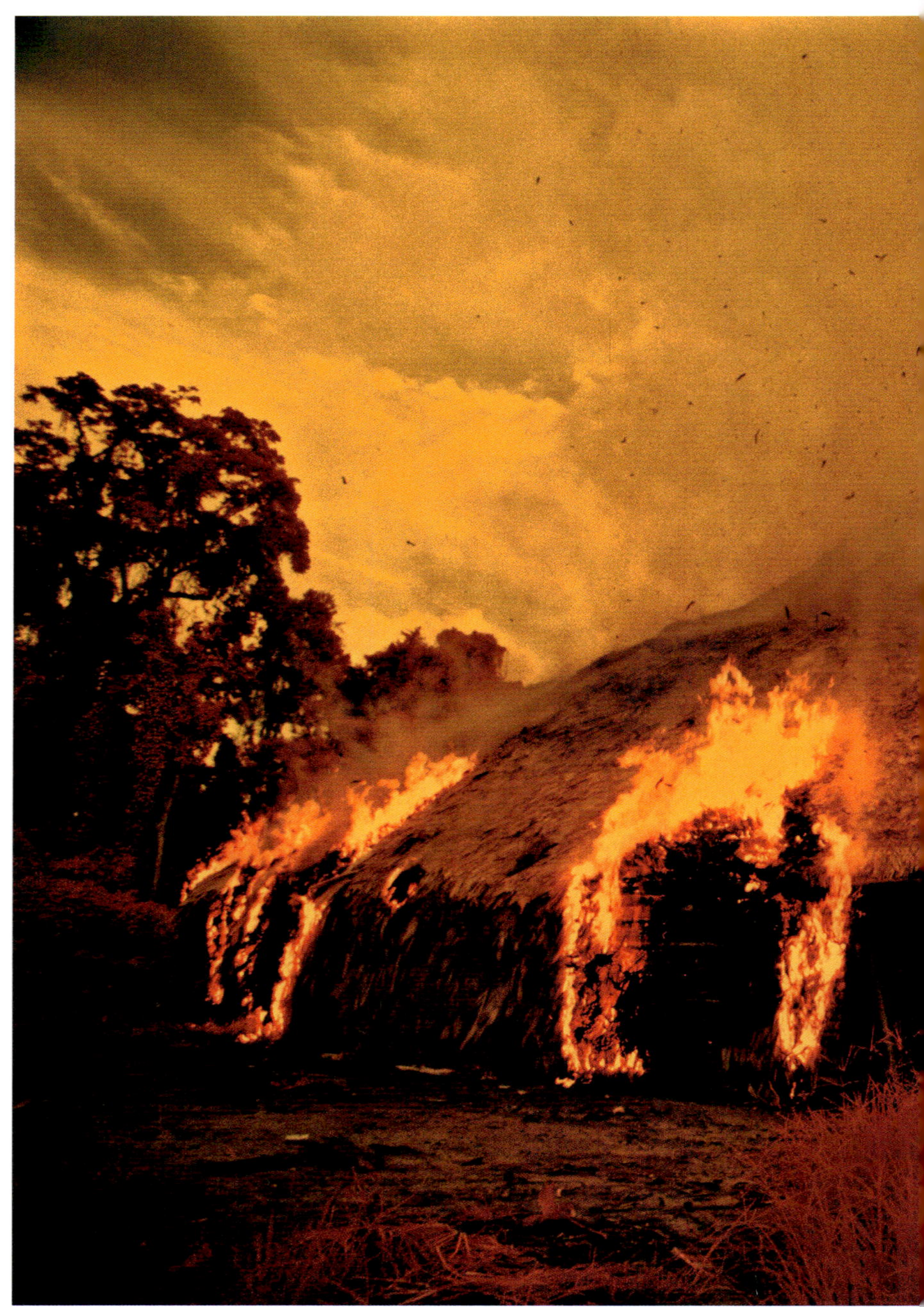

   Hut in flames

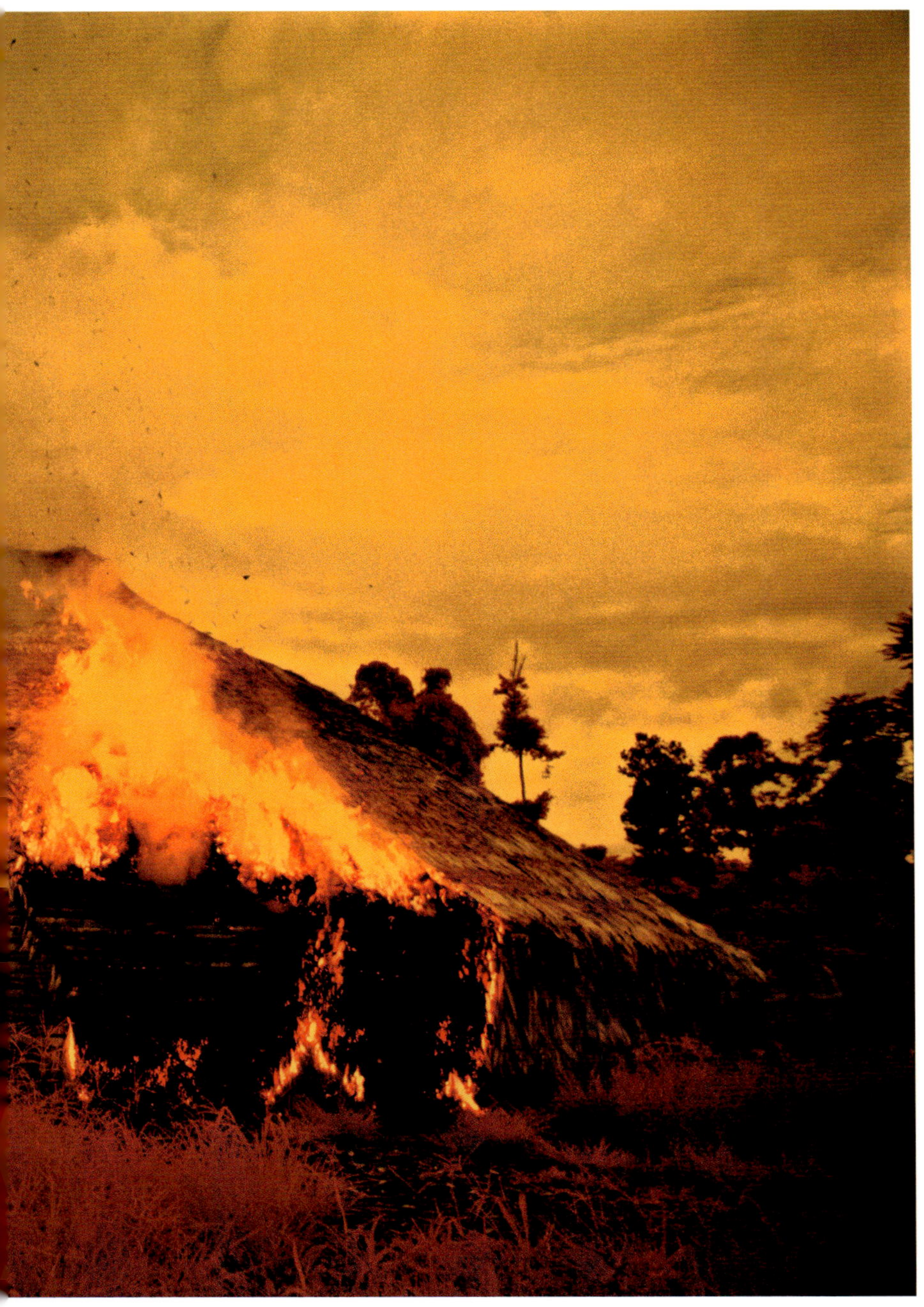

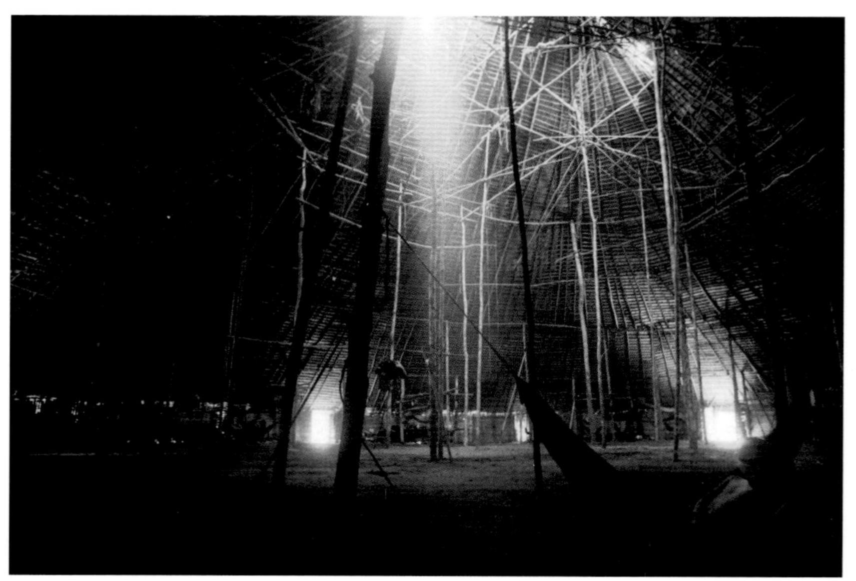

24   Untitled 1981–3

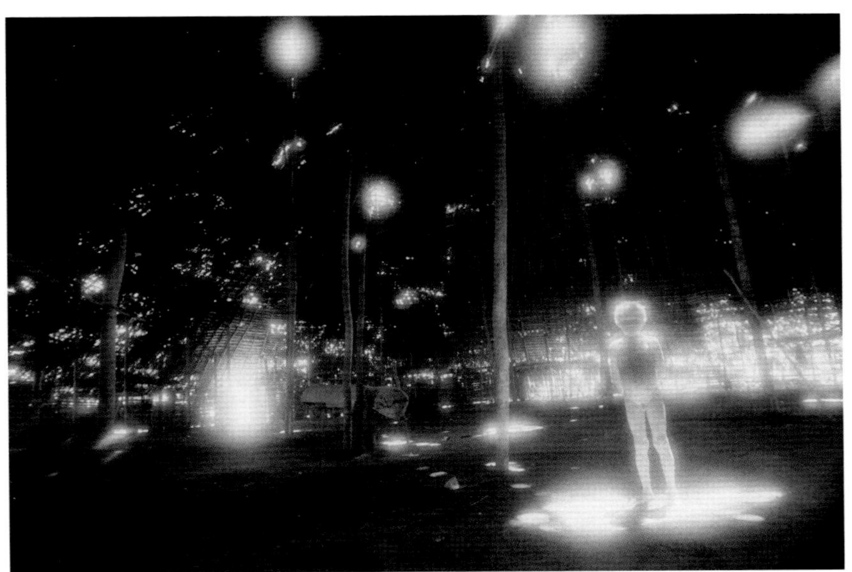

    Yanomami

MARCADOS (MARKED) 1981–3

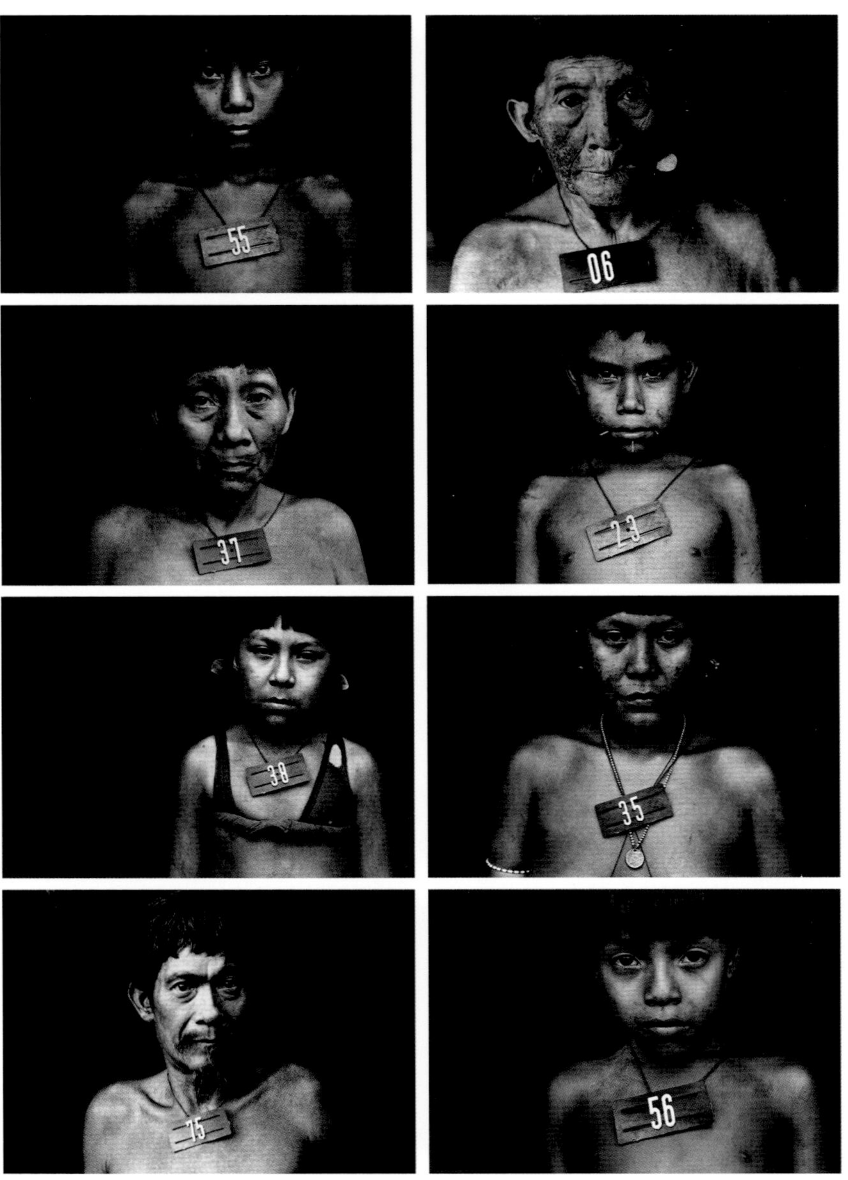

 Horizontal 1

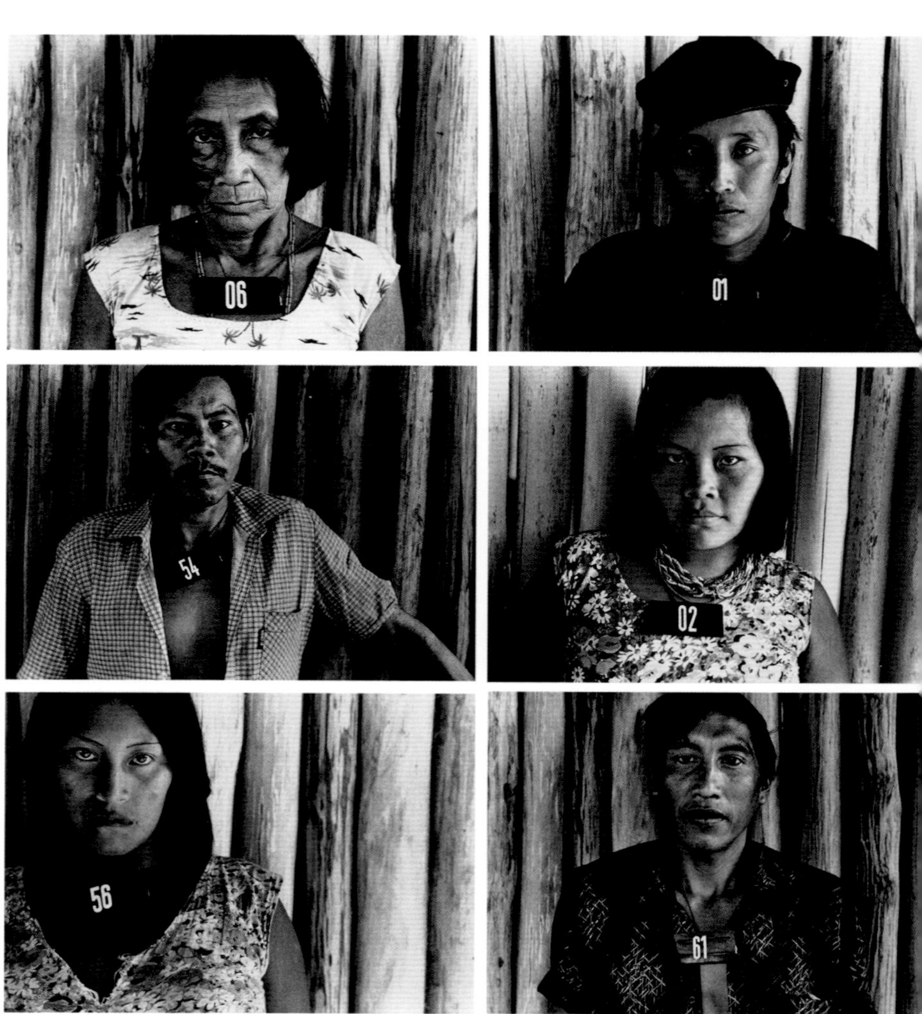

     Horizontal 2

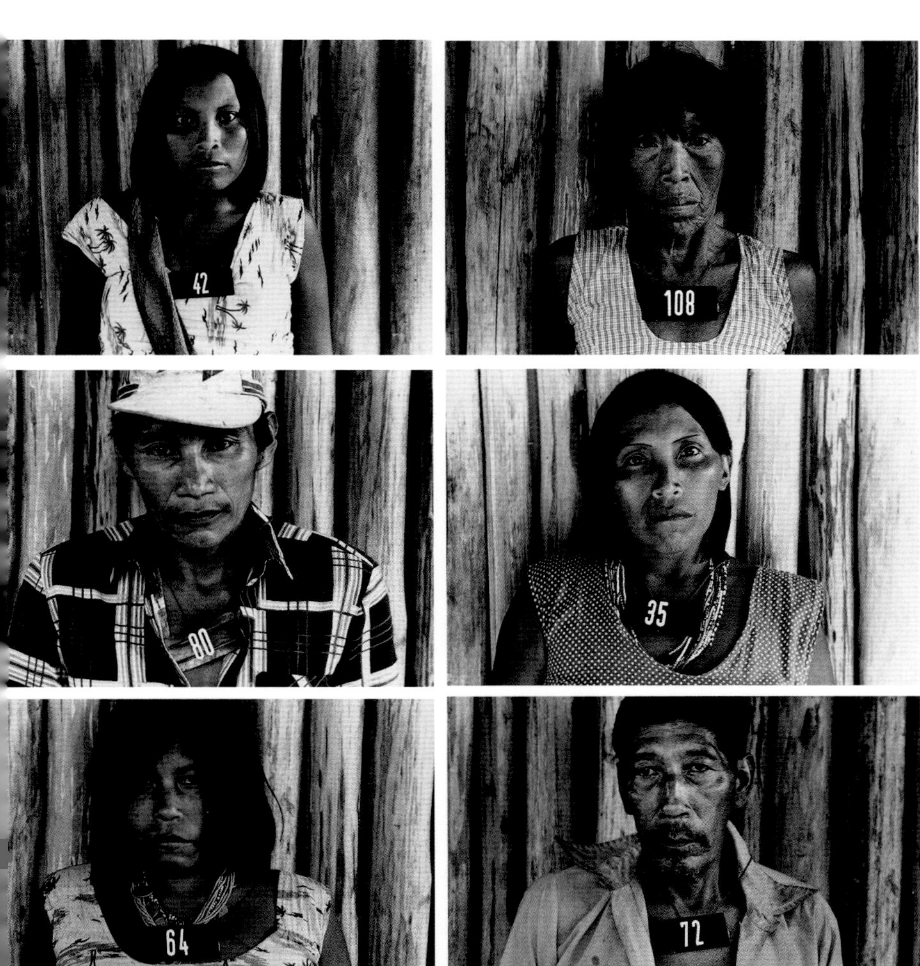

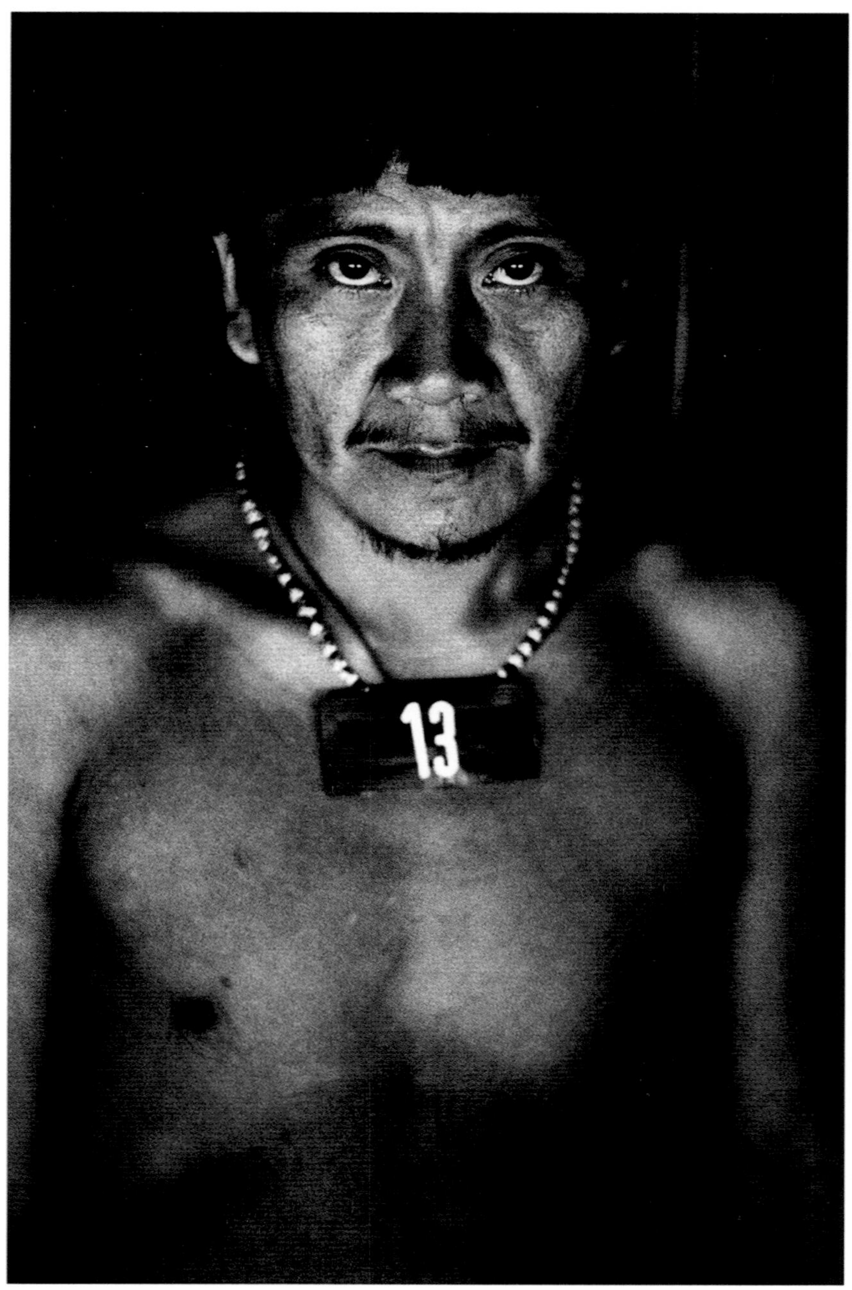

     Vertical 8 (details)

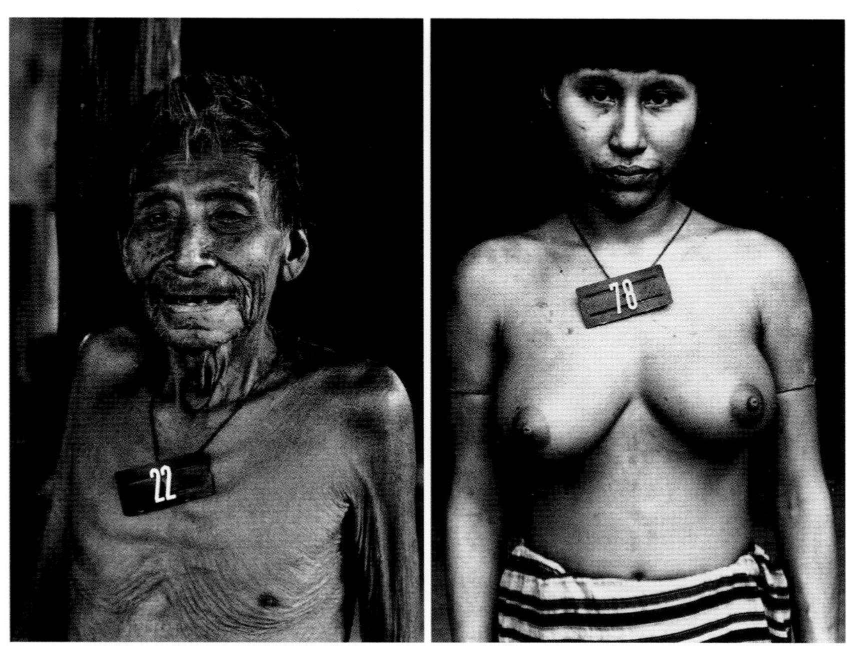

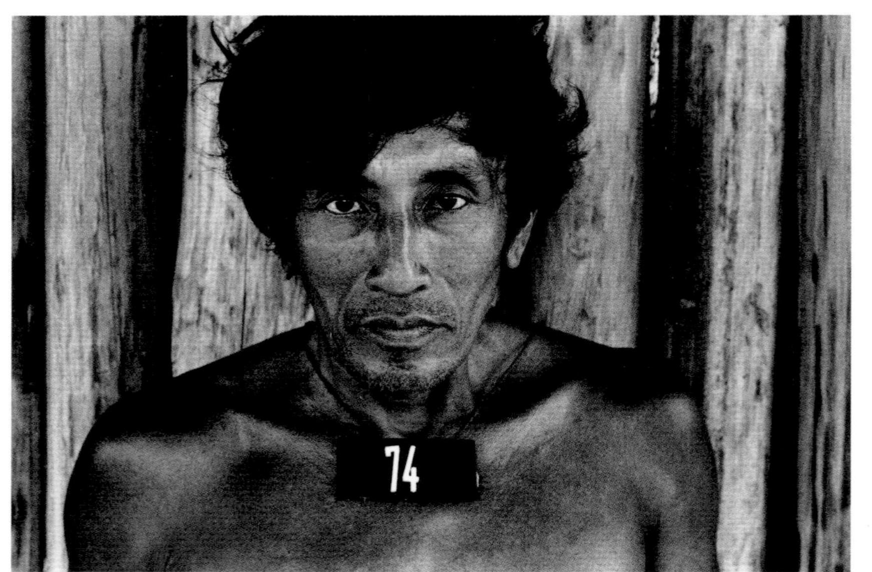

 Horizontal 6 (detail)

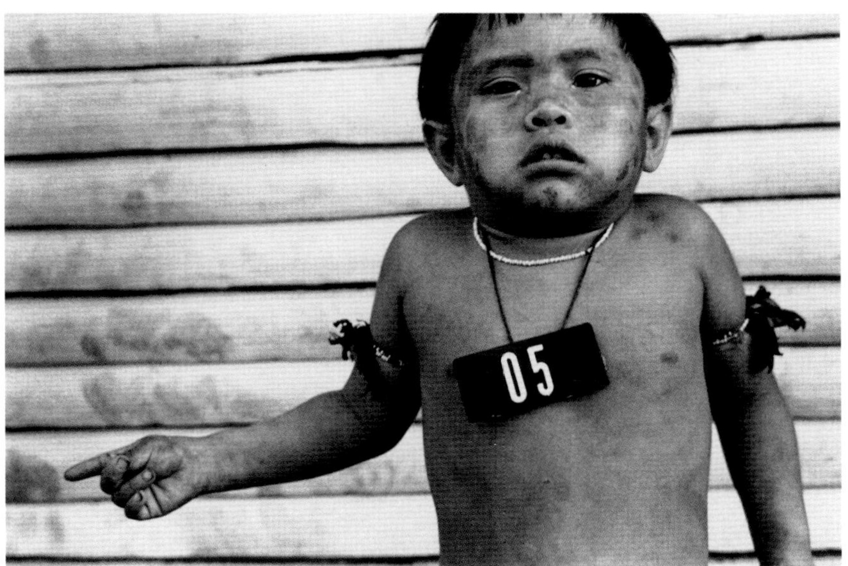

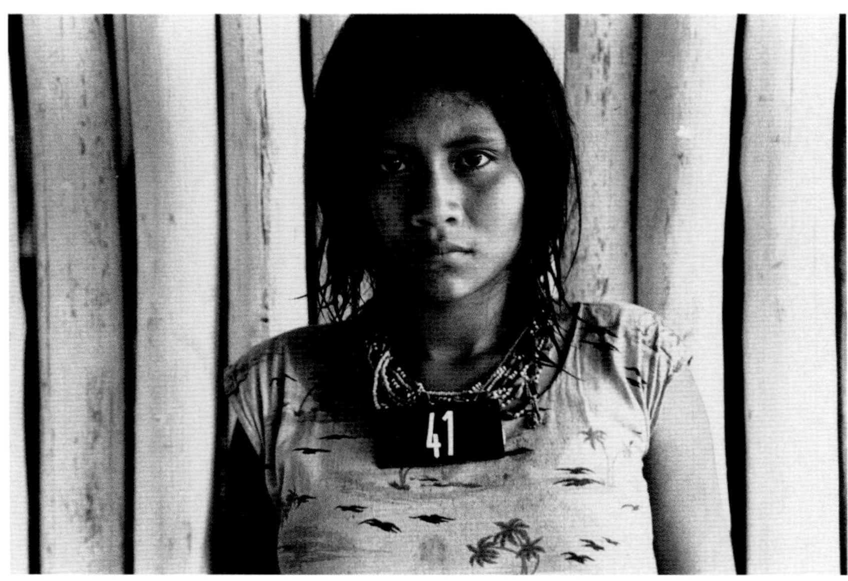

Above: *Horizontal 6* (details)
Overleaf: *Vertical 10*

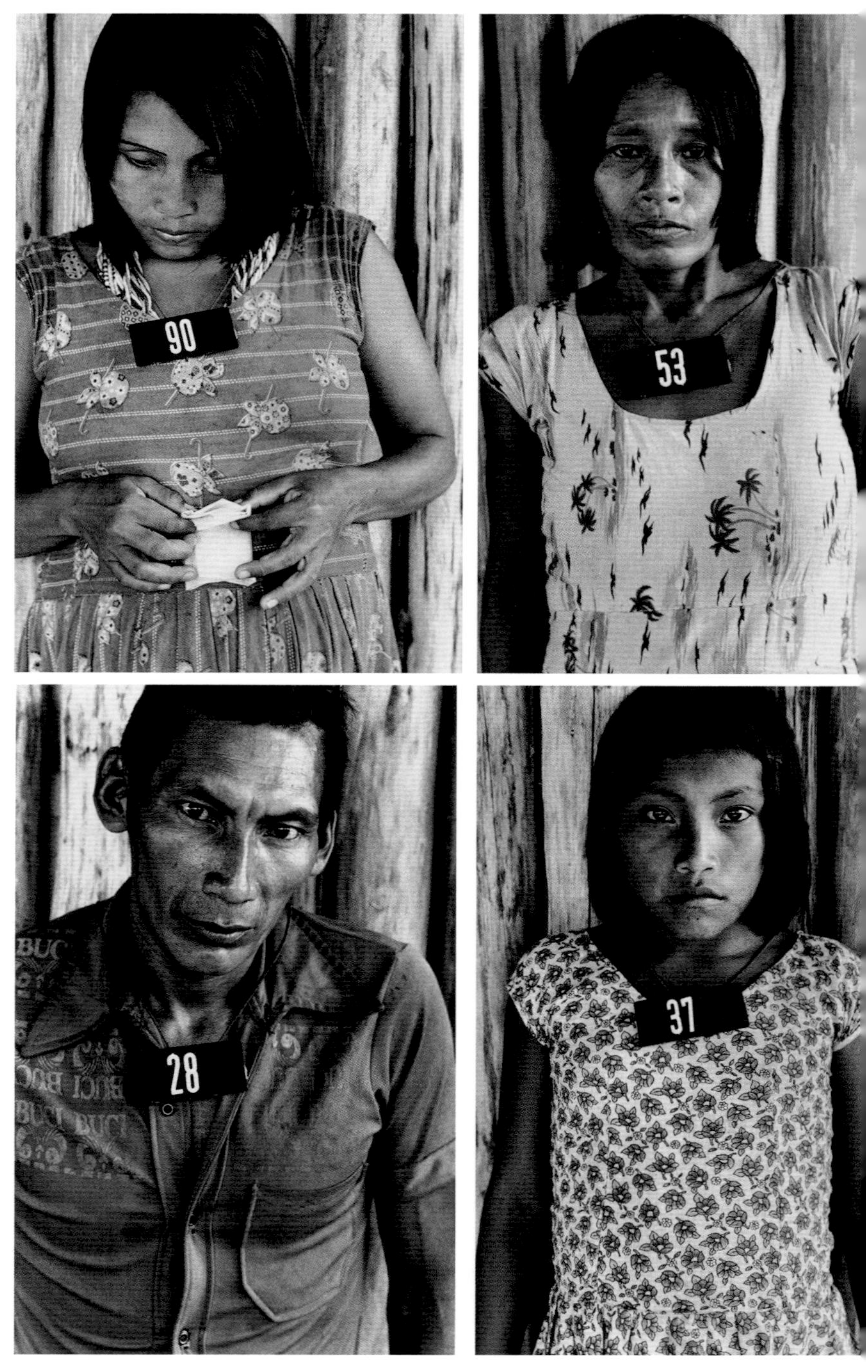

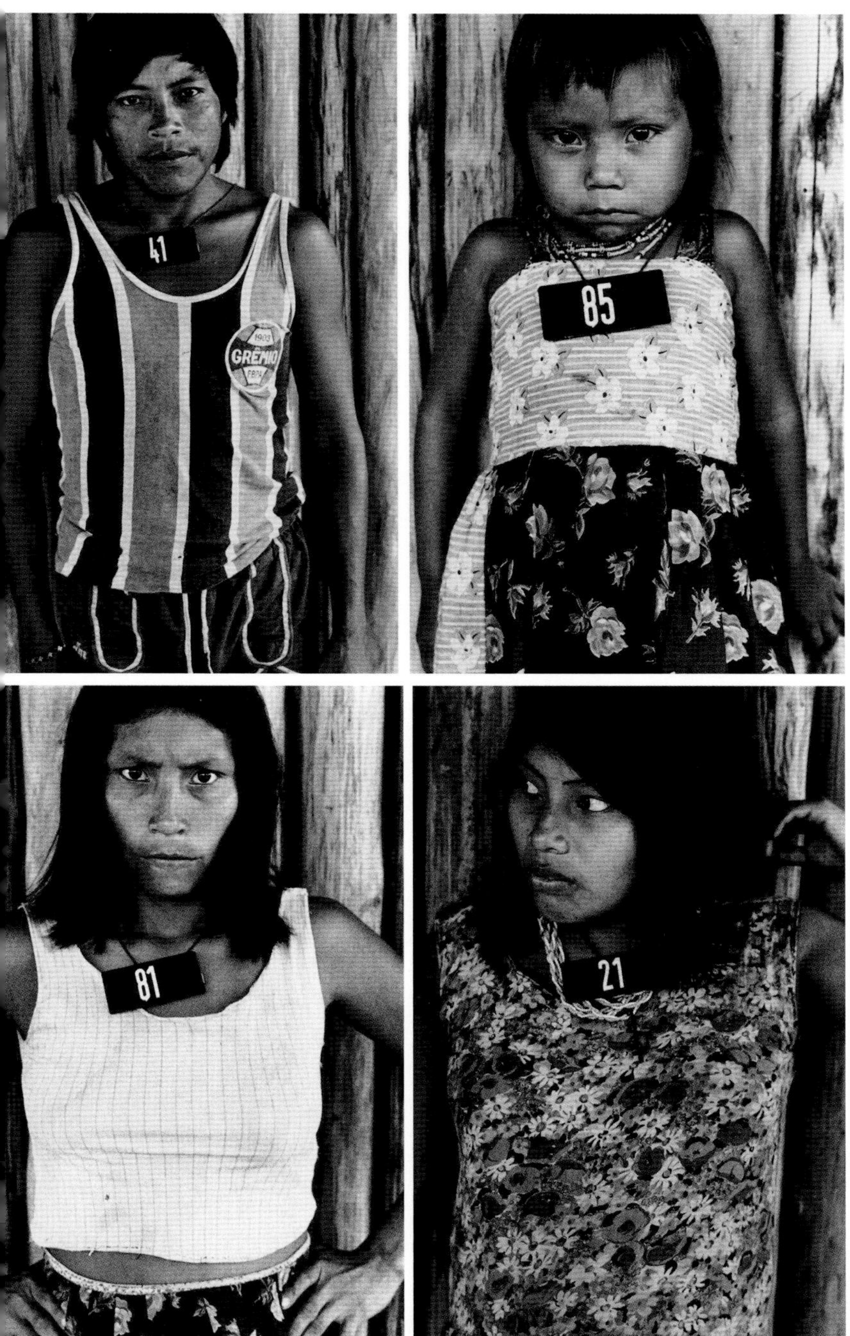

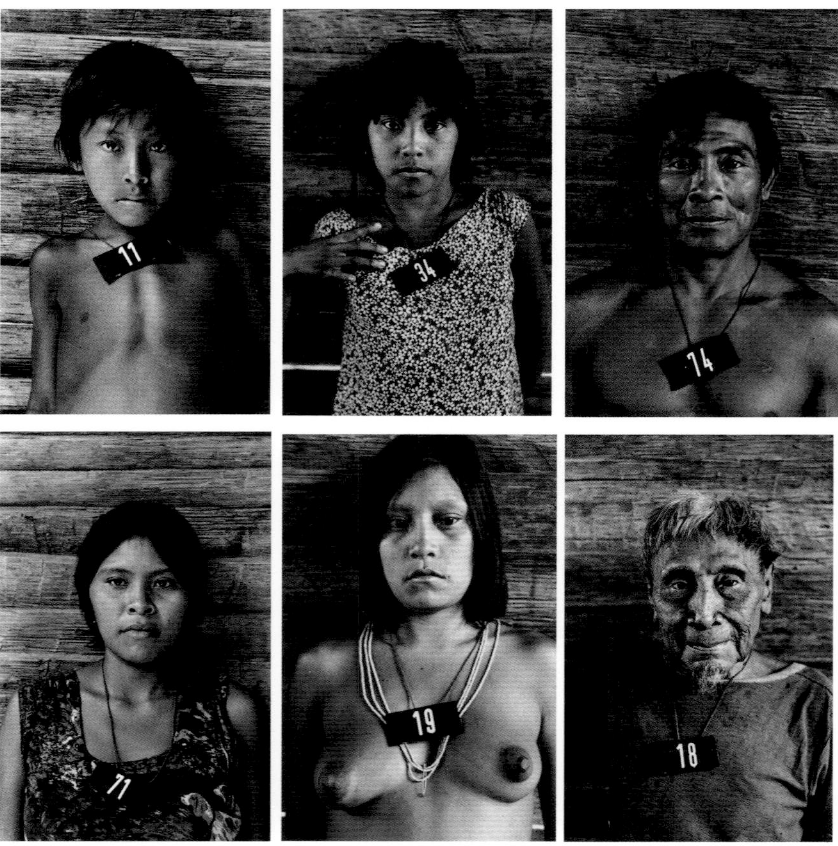

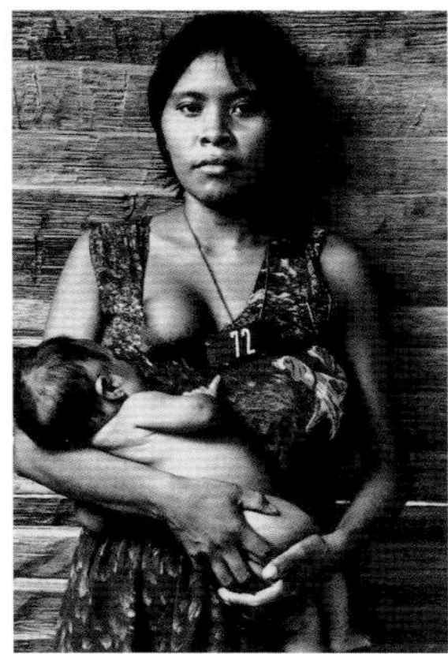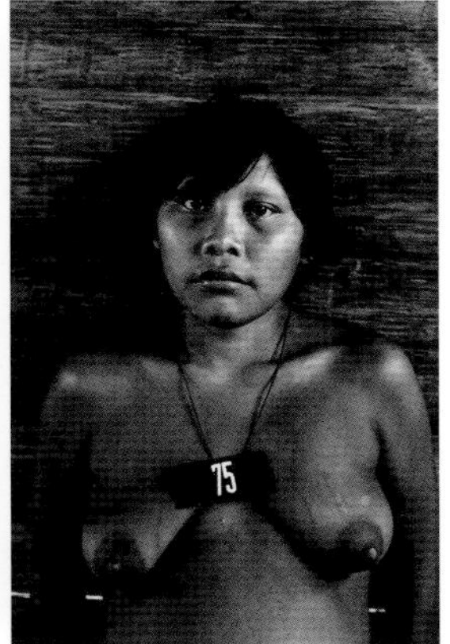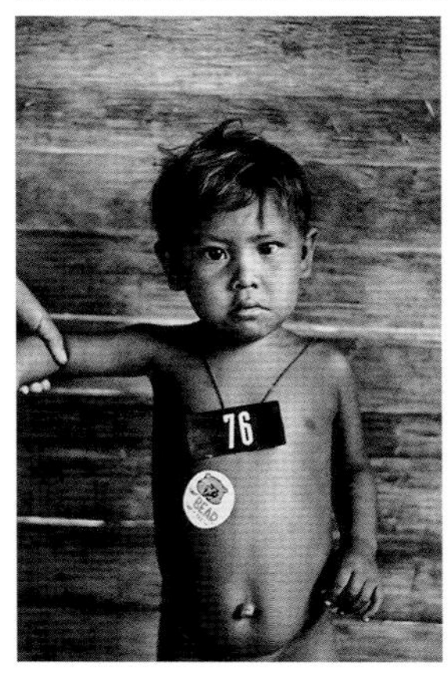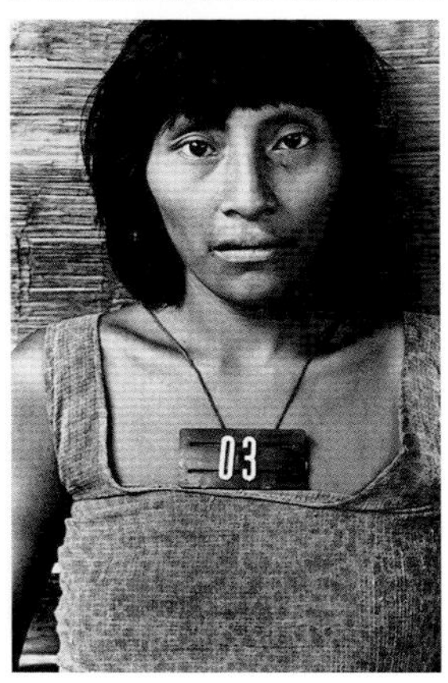

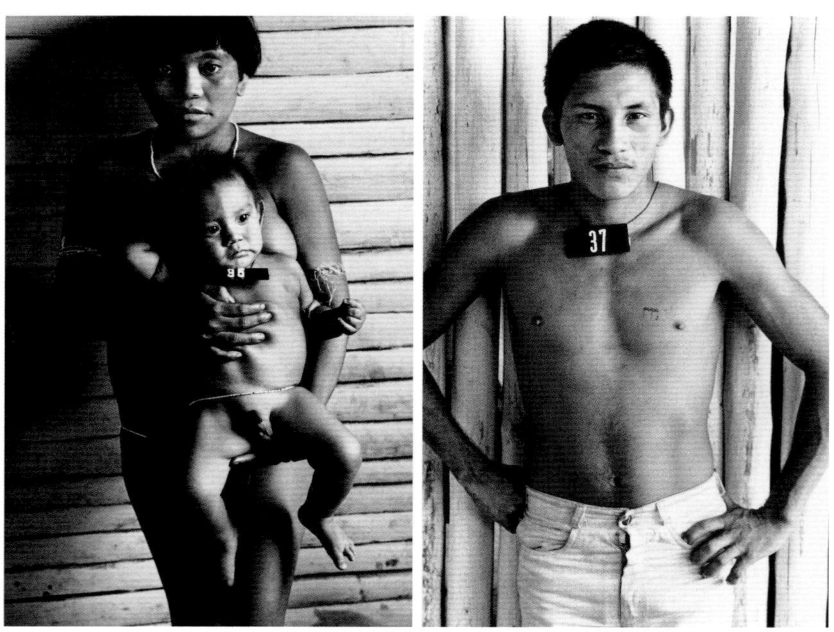

   Vertical 14 (details)

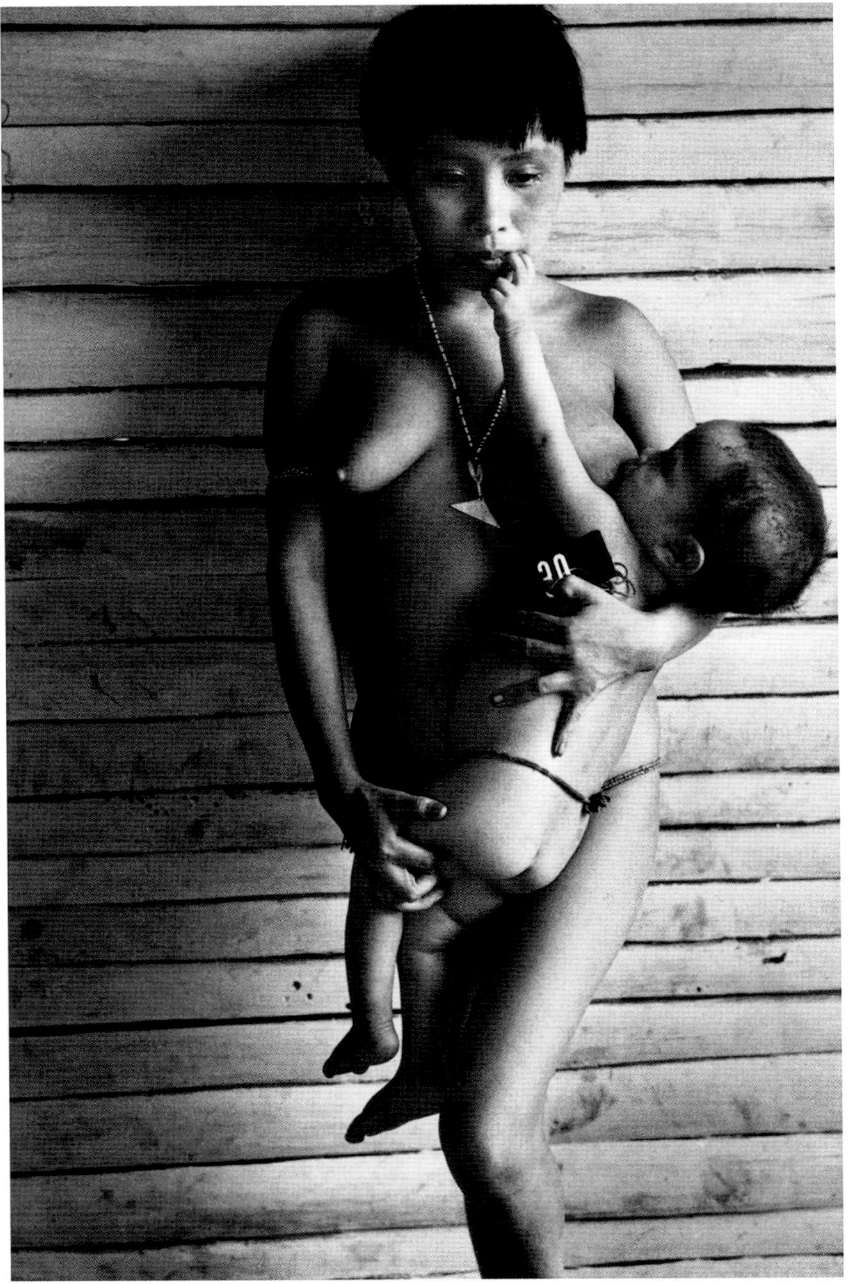

SONHOS (DREAMS) 2002

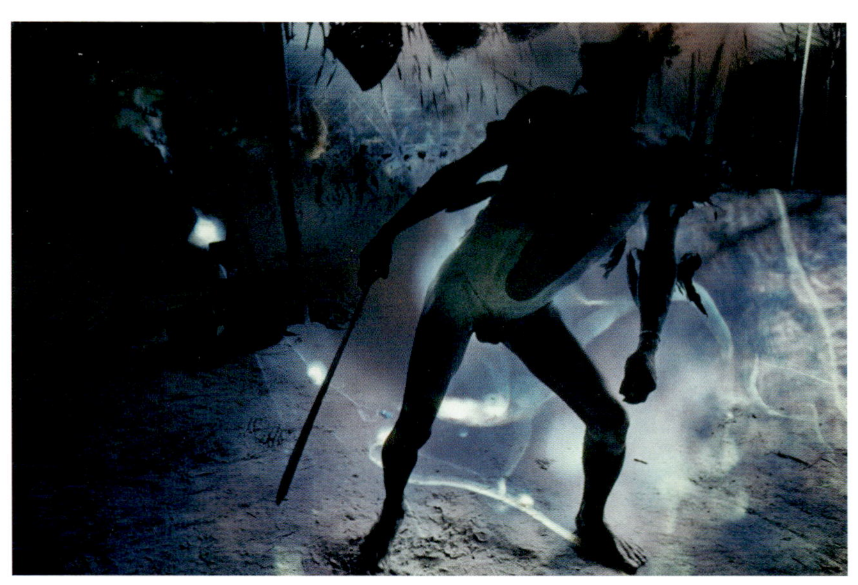

      Warrior from Toototobi

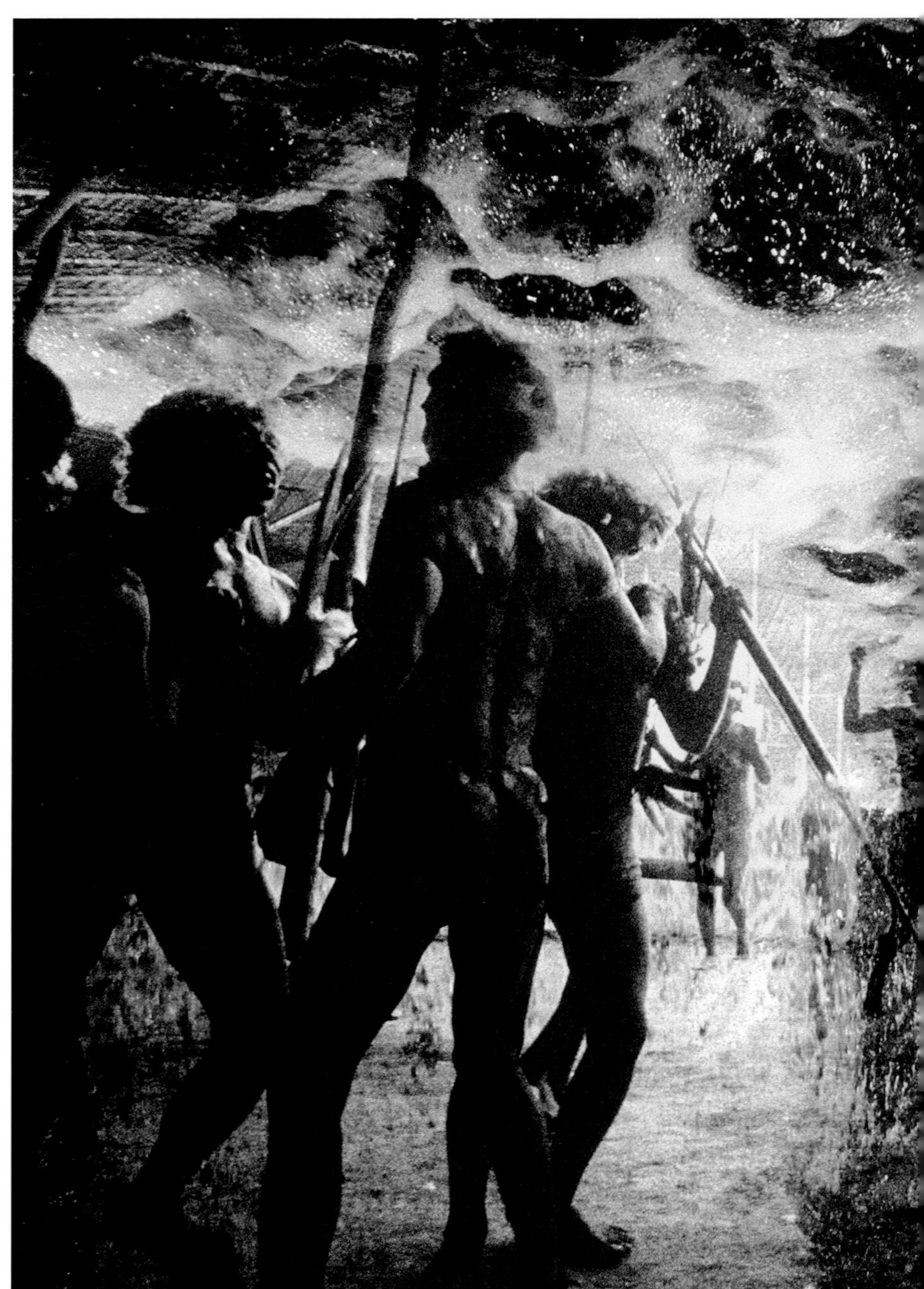

   Falling sky / The end of the world

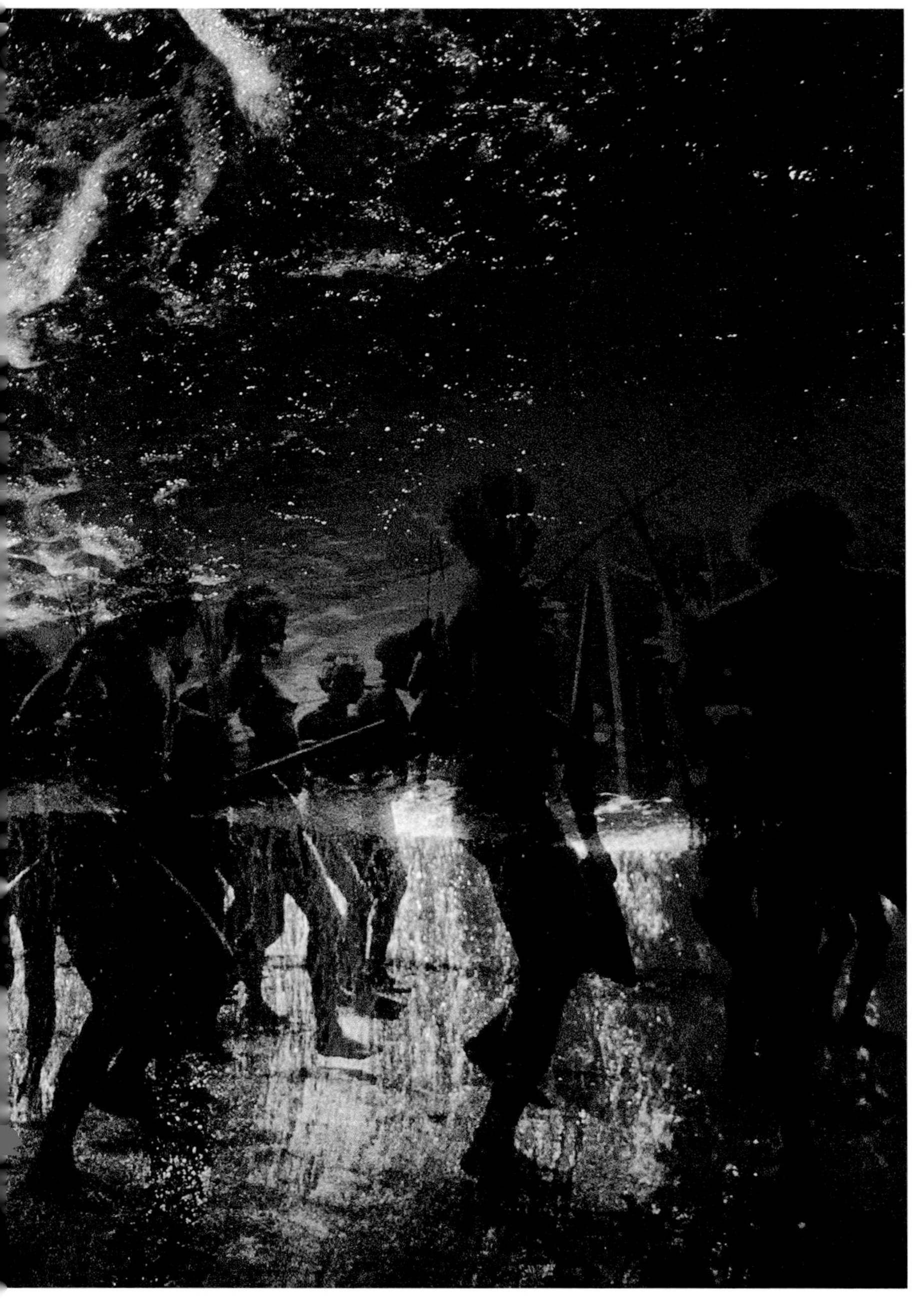

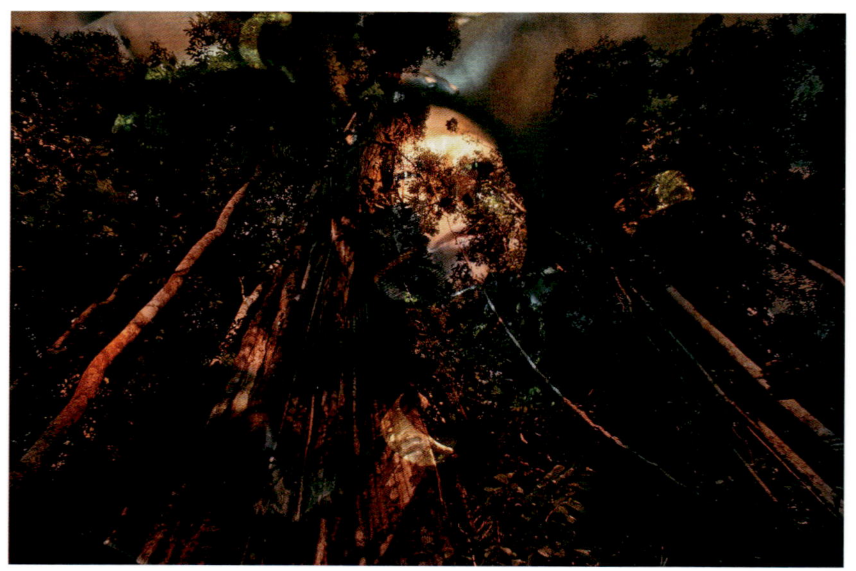

Amazon rainforest, Pará

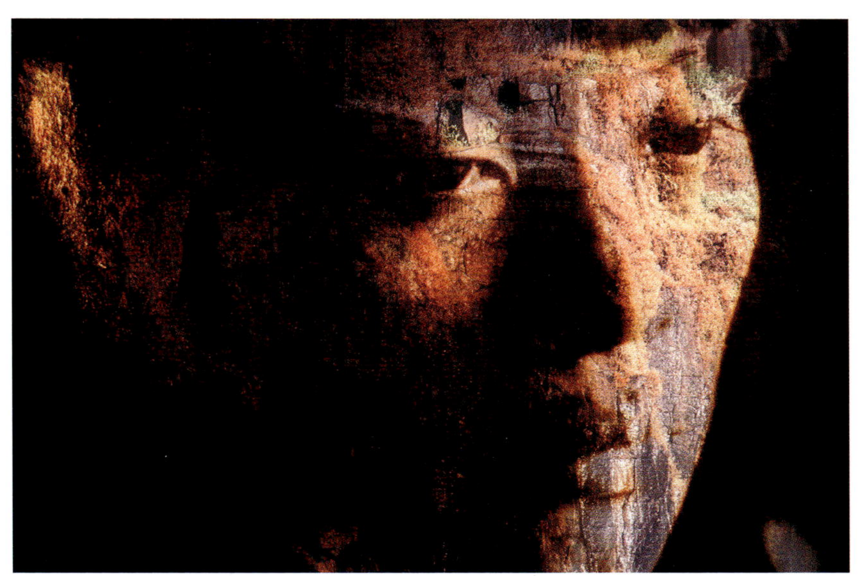

    Hélio for the whites

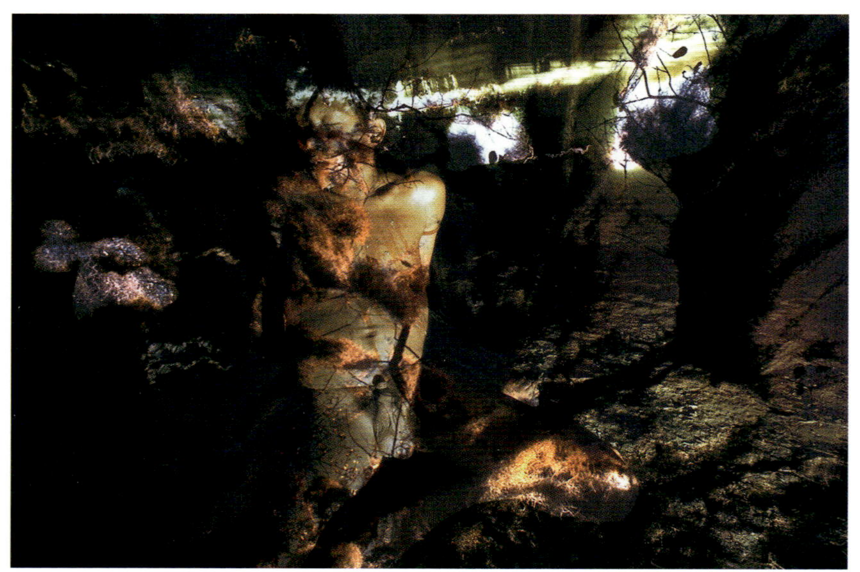

   Youngster in a trance

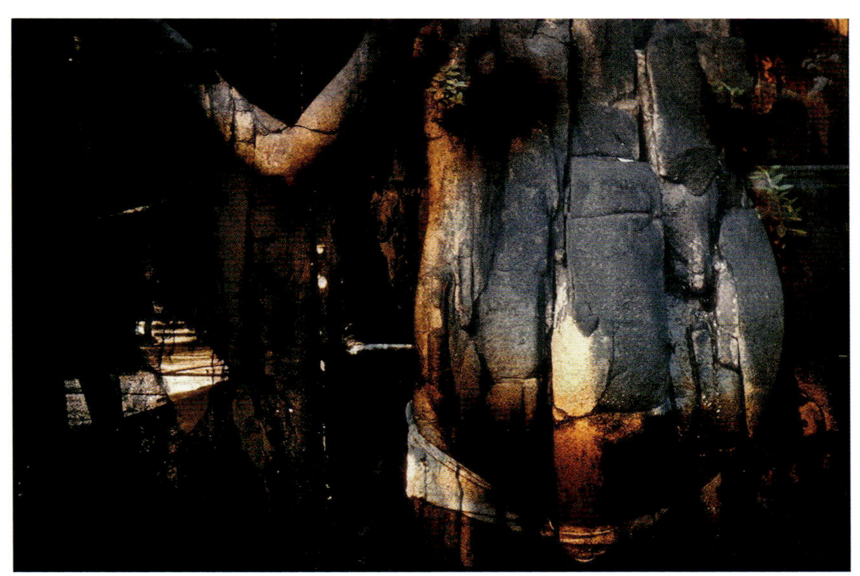

   Young pregnant woman

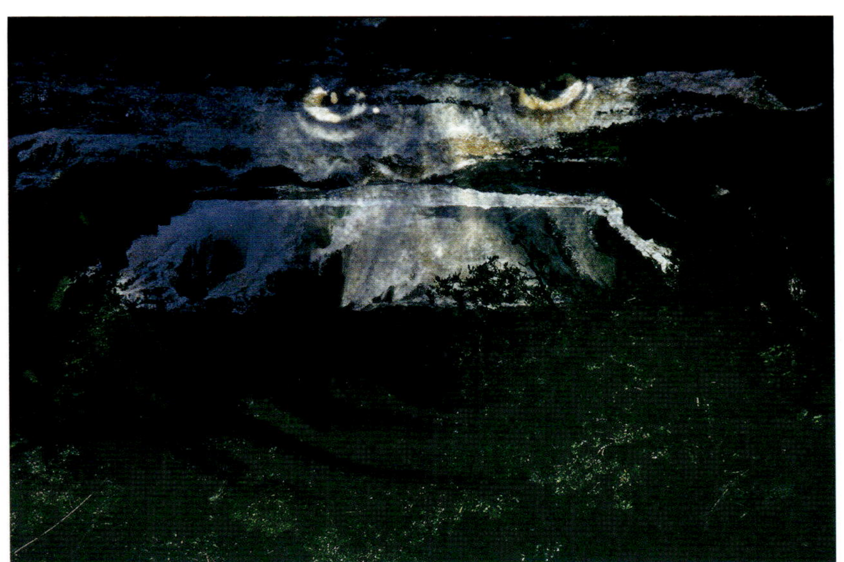

49   *Spirit of the Forest*

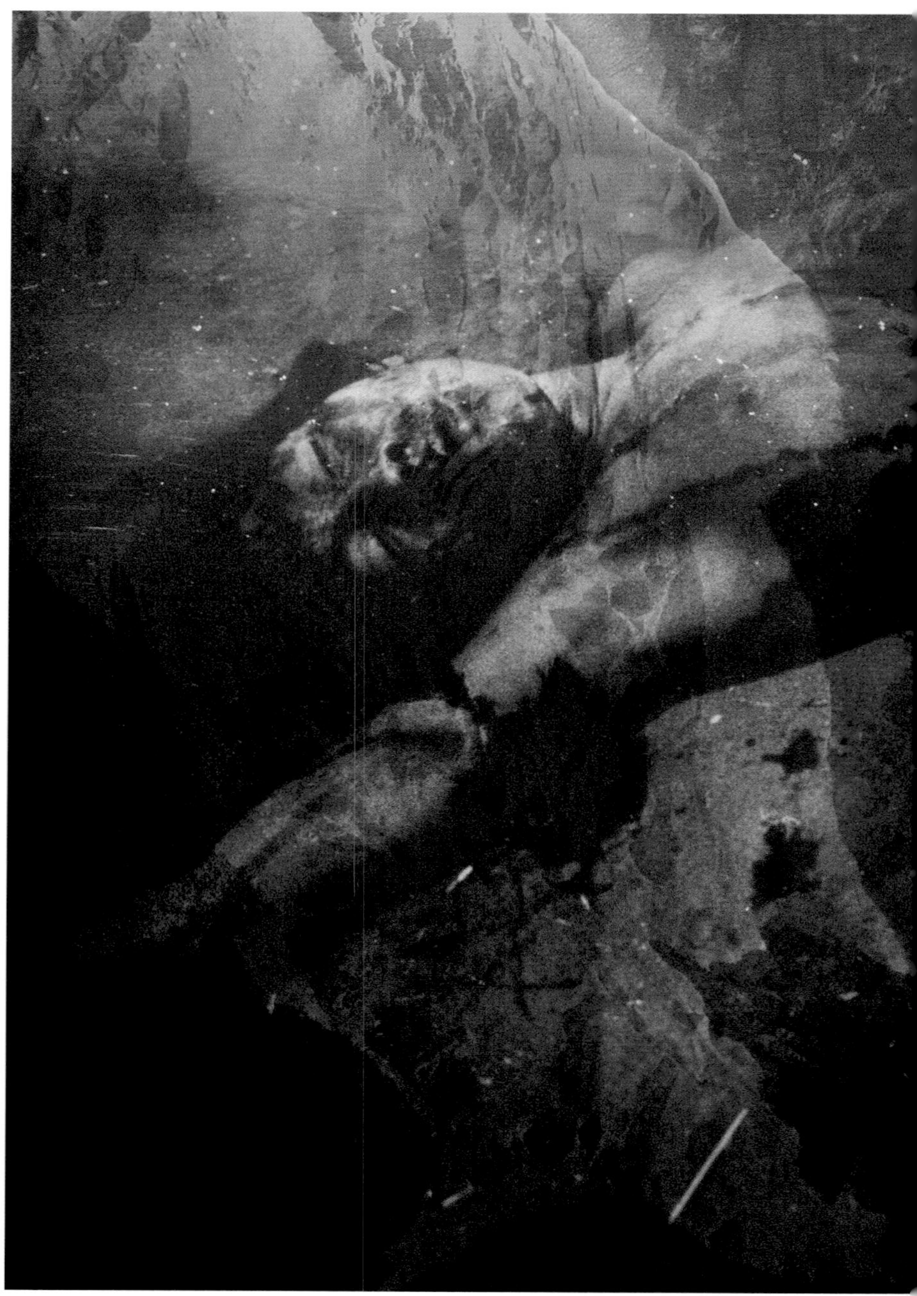

     Ecstasy

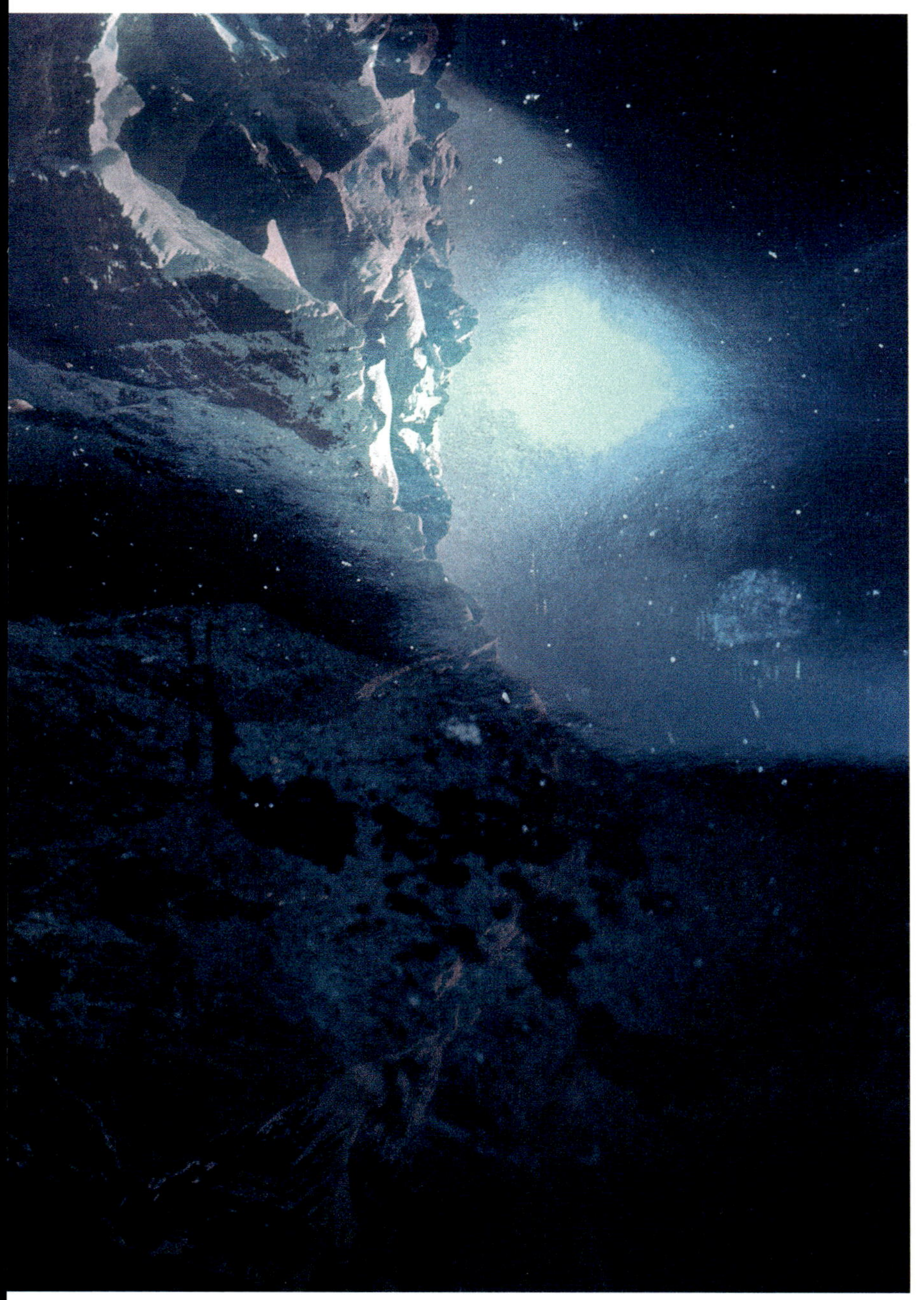

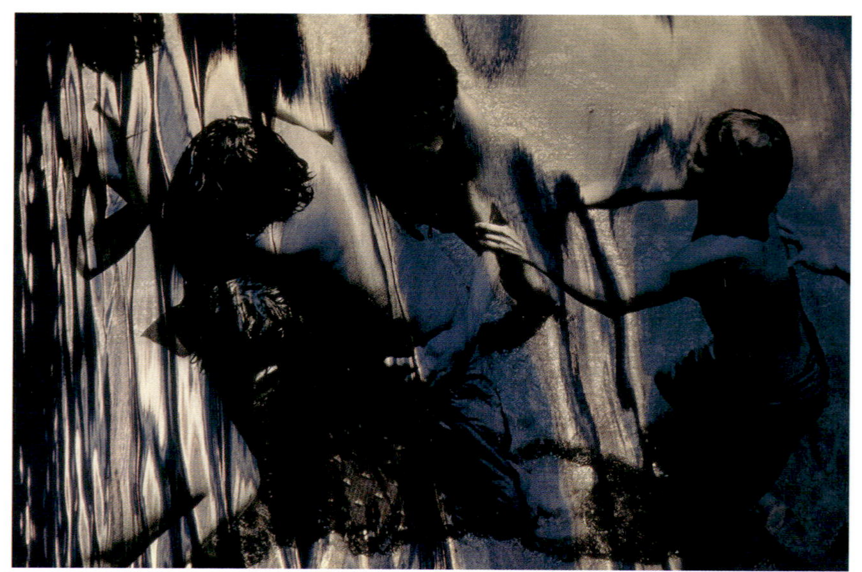

    The power of water

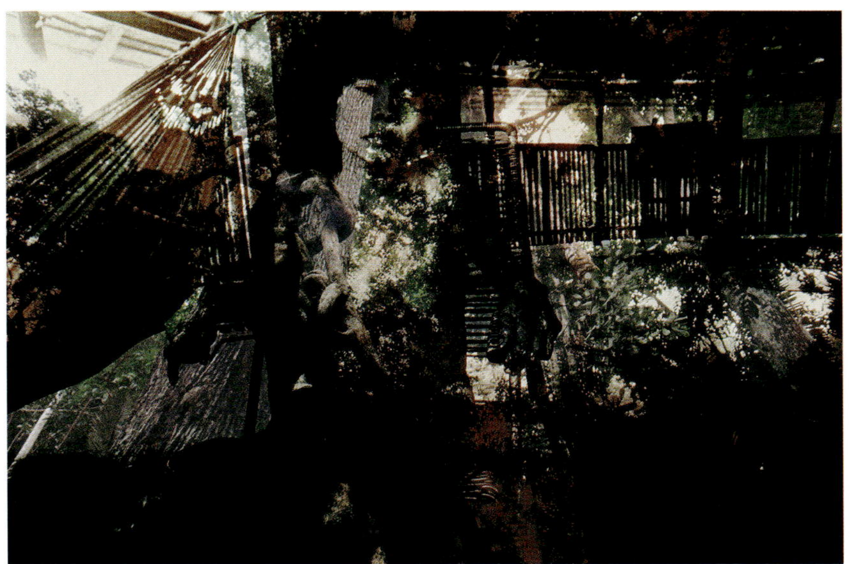

    Rest

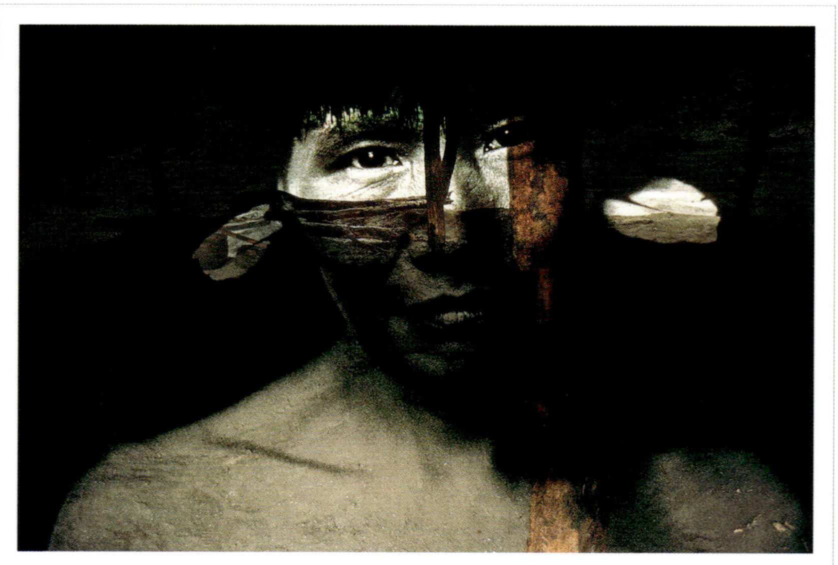

Opiq+theri, Perimetral norte

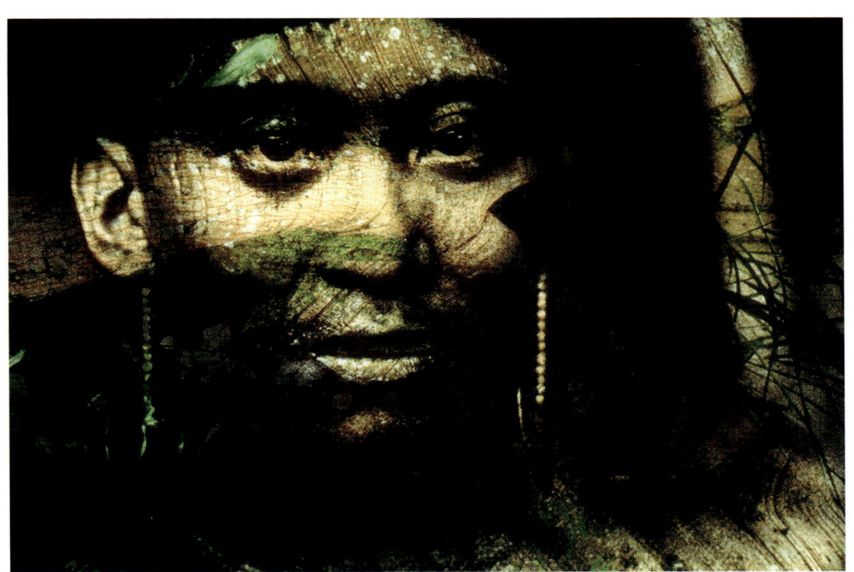

55 *Reahu in Toototobi*

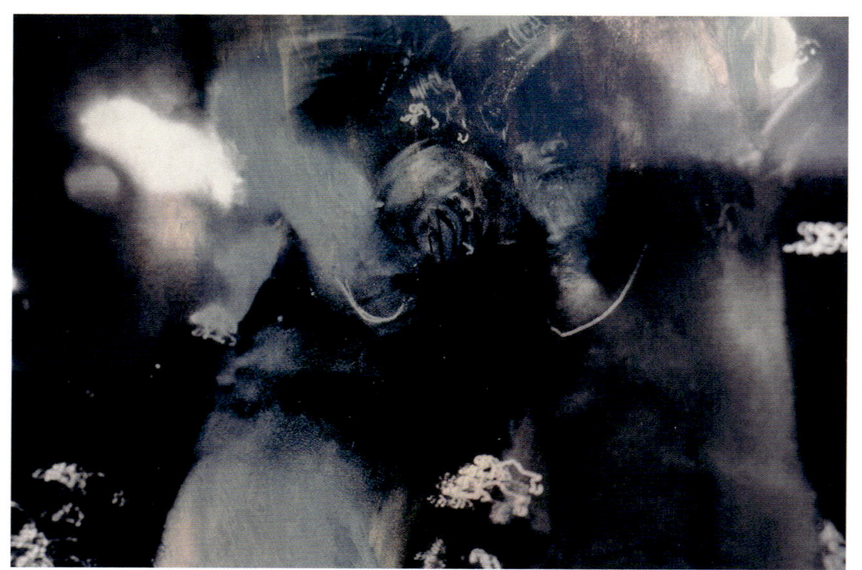

    Untitled

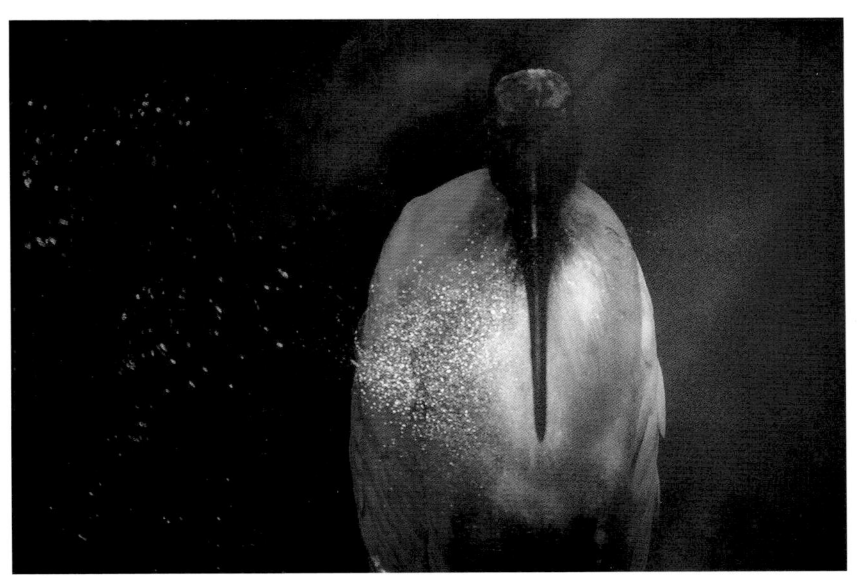

57   Untitled

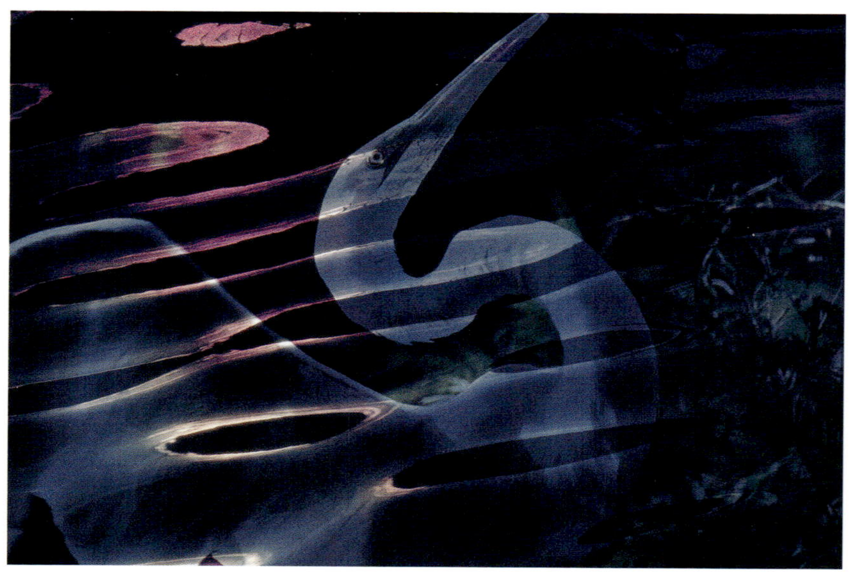

58　Untitled

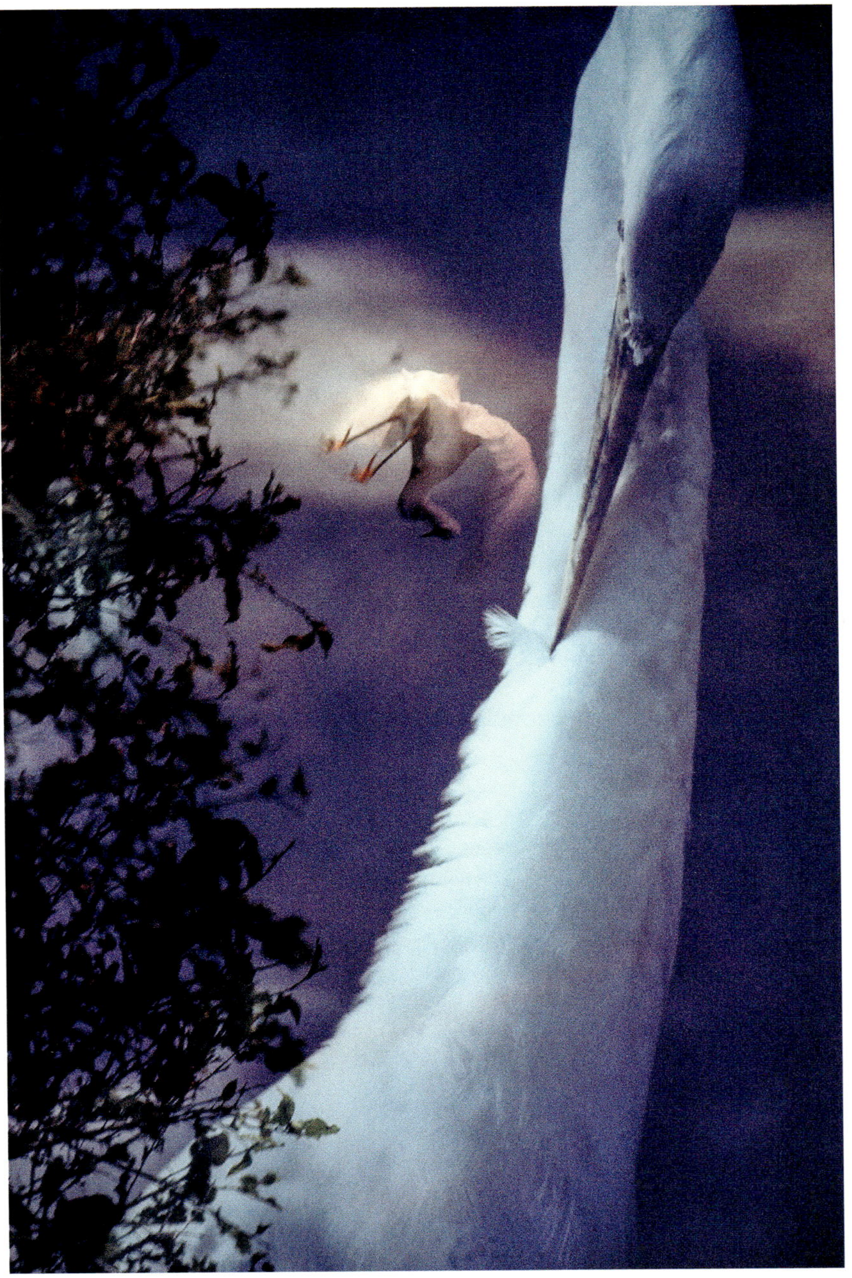

Untitled

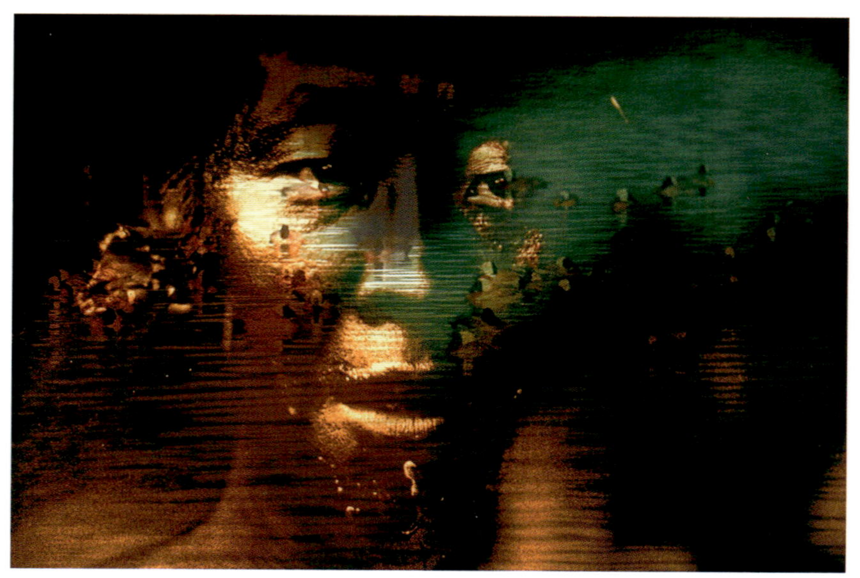

60   *The song of the waters*

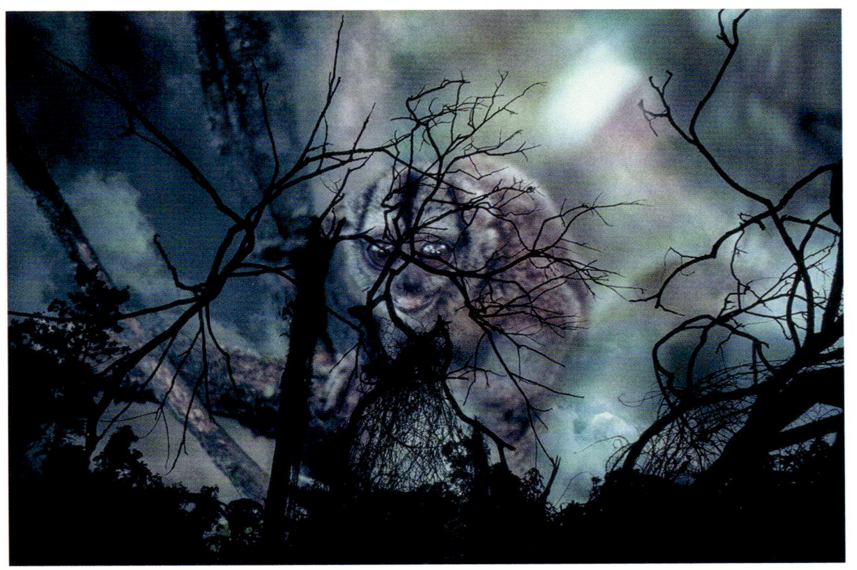

 Untitled

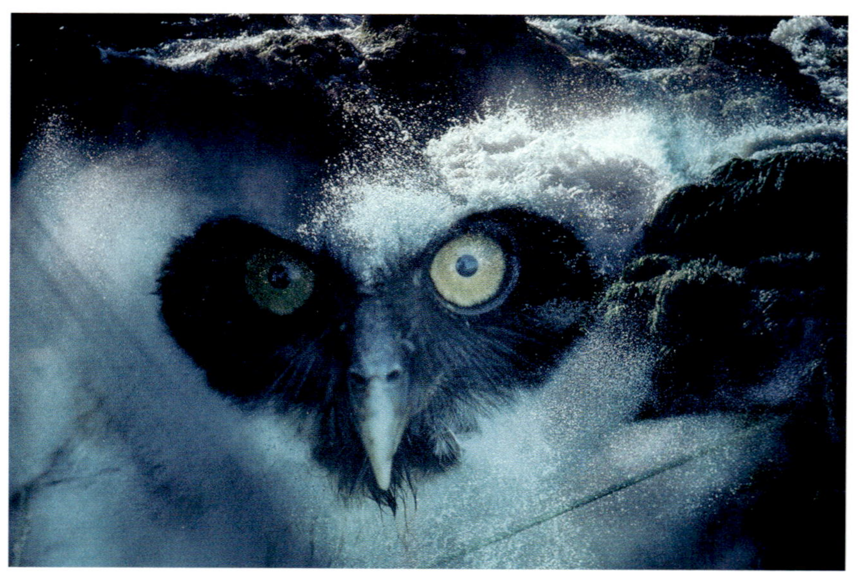

    Untitled

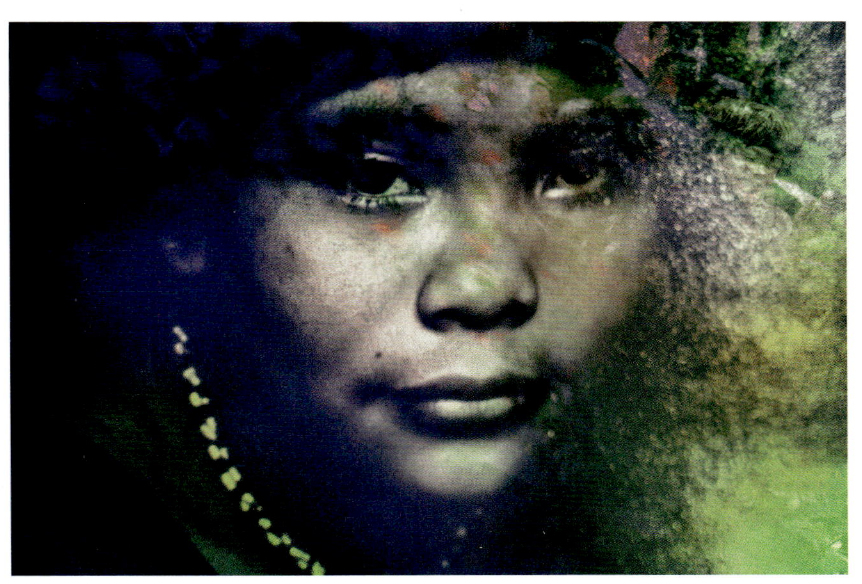

63   *Bluish green*

CREDITS

All artworks © Claudia Andujar, courtesy
Galeria Vermelho